AMERICAN SUMMER
COOKBOOK

TASTE OF HOME BOOKS • RDA ENTHUSIAST BRANDS, LLC • MILWAUKEE, WI

Visit us at tasteofhome.com for other
Taste of Home books and products.

International Standard Book Number:
978-1-62145-858-6

Component Number:
116700113H

Executive Editor: Mark Hagen
Senior Art Director: Raeann Thompson
Art Director: Courtney Lovetere
Deputy Editor, Copy Desk: Dulcie Shoener
Copy Editor: Cathy Jakicic
Contributing Designer: Jennifer Ruetz

Cover Photography
Photographer: Grace Natoli Sheldon
Senior Set Stylist: Melissa Franco
Senior Food Stylist: Shannon Roum

Pictured on front cover:
All-American Hamburgers, p. 61;
Mama's Warm German Potato Salad, p. 21; and
Marinated Mozzarella & Tomato Appetizers, p. 12

Pictured on title page:
Honey Hydrator, p. 9;
Spiced Pulled Pork Sandwiches, p. 73;
Peach-Chipotle Baby Back Ribs, p. 84; and
Berry-Patch Brownie Pizza, p. 107

Pictured on back cover:
Grilled Green Beans, p. 34;
Sweet & Tangy Barbecued Chicken, p. 83; and
Star-Spangled Lemon Icebox Pie, p. 111

INSTANT POT is a trademark of Double Insight Inc.
This publication has not been authorized, sponsored
or otherwise approved by Double Insight Inc.

Printed in USA
1 3 5 7 9 10 8 6 4 2

ALL-AMERICAN
HAMBURGERS, P. 61

MORE WAYS TO CONNECT WITH US:

DIG IN TO SUMMER!

Turn here for summer's best food, flavor and fun! Serve up everything from juicy burgers and savory steaks to frosty treats and desserts made brilliant with fresh berries. You'll find dozens of the season's best beverages, appetizers, main courses, sides and desserts in this incredible collection.

AT-A-GLANCE ICONS

FAST FIX: Prepare these recipes, start to finish, in 30 minutes or less.

5 INGREDIENTS: These dishes call for just a few ingredients. (We don't count water, salt, pepper, oils and optional items such as garnishes.)

FREEZE IT: These recipes freeze beautifully. Stock your freezer with these specialties to save time later.

SLOW COOKER: Put your favorite kitchen tool to work with dishes that simmer to perfection on their own.

THIS ULTIMATE GUIDE TO SUMMER INCLUDES:

• 154 no-fuss recipes that celebrate the tastiest time of year

• Complete party menus for hosting impressive get-togethers all season long

• Tips from our Test Kitchen that speed meal prep and inspiring full-color photos

• An entire section of Instant Pot® and air-fryer dishes perfect for keeping the kitchen cool

• Recipes that use just 5 ingredients or are table-ready in half an hour or less

• Complete nutrition facts with every recipe and diabetic exchanges where applicable

Take a big bite out of the best season of the year! It's never been more delicious than with the *Taste of Home American Summer Cookbook.*

CONTENTS:

SUMMER'S CLASSIC

APPETIZERS & BEVERAGES

From pool parties and backyard barbecues to church picnics and pregame tailgates, summer snacking is a snap when you take advantage of all the refreshing flavors this season has to offer.

COCONUT CHICKEN & SHRIMP

I was looking for a fun, easy weeknight dinner that was based on our favorite shrimp dish and healthier than fast food. This has become a favorite!
—Susan Seymour, Valatie, NY

PREP: 30 MIN. • **COOK:** 5 MIN./BATCH
MAKES: 6 SERVINGS

- 1 cup all-purpose flour
- 1 cup lime-flavored seltzer water
- 1 tsp. ground ginger
- 1 tsp. salt
- 1 tsp. pepper
- 2½ cups sweetened shredded coconut
- 1¼ cups panko bread crumbs
- 1 lb. uncooked shrimp (31-40 per lb.), peeled and deveined
- 2 boneless skinless chicken breasts (6 oz. each), cut into ¾-in. cubes
  Oil for deep-fat frying
  Optional: Additional salt and pepper and lime wedges

MAUI MUSTARD
- 1 can (8 oz.) crushed pineapple, well drained
- ½ cup red pepper jelly
- 3 Tbsp. stone-ground mustard

1. In a shallow bowl, whisk together first 5 ingredients. In another shallow bowl, combine coconut and panko. Dip shrimp in batter to coat. Dip in coconut mixture, patting to help coating adhere. Repeat with chicken.
2. In an electric skillet or deep fryer, heat oil to 350°. Fry shrimp, a few at a time, until golden brown, 3-4 minutes. Drain on paper towels. Repeat with the chicken. If desired, sprinkle lightly with salt and pepper.
3. For mustard, mix together pineapple, pepper jelly and stone-ground mustard. Combine shrimp and chicken; serve with mustard and, if desired, lime wedges.
1 serving: 659 cal., 31g fat (14g sat. fat), 123mg chol., 735mg sod., 69g carb. (39g sugars, 4g fiber), 29g pro.

In the mood for just seafood? Skip the chicken and add more shrimp.

GRILLED PEACH & PINEAPPLE SANGRIA

GRILLED PEACH & PINEAPPLE SANGRIA

Grill up a few fresh peaches and some pineapple slathered in cinnamon butter and make a refreshing summer sangria. I also like to add slices of grilled lemon and lime to the glass for a boost of citrus flavor.
—Heather King, Frostburg, MD

PREP: 25 MIN. + CHILLING
MAKES: 8 SERVINGS

- 1 bottle (750 ml) sauvignon blanc or other white wine
- 2 cups lemonade
- ½ cup orange liqueur
- 1 Tbsp. butter, melted
- 1 Tbsp. sugar
- 1 tsp. ground cinnamon
- 3 medium peeled peaches, pitted and halved
- ¼ fresh pineapple, peeled and cut into 4 slices

1. Make sangria by combining wine, lemonade and liqueur. Refrigerate. Meanwhile, in a small bowl, combine melted butter, sugar and cinnamon. Mix well.
2. Brush butter mixture over cut side of peaches and all over pineapple slices. Grill fruit, covered, on a greased rack over medium direct heat 4-5 minutes. Turn the peaches and pineapple. Grill 4-5 minutes more. Remove from grill.
3. Cut each peach half into 5 or 6 slices and each of the pineapple slices into 5 or 6 pieces. Add three-fourths of the fruit to sangria, reserving the remainder. Refrigerate at least 2 hours.
4. Before serving, thread several pieces of reserved fruit onto appetizer skewers. Pour sangria over ice; serve with the fruit skewers.
¾ cup: 206 cal., 2g fat (1g sat. fat), 4mg chol., 20mg sod., 25g carb. (21g sugars, 1g fiber), 1g pro.

BASIL CITRUS COCKTAIL

This irresistible cocktail is fruity, fantastic and low in calories!
—*Taste of Home* Test Kitchen

TAKES: 10 MIN. • **MAKES:** 1 SERVING

- 6 fresh basil leaves
- 1½ to 2 cups ice cubes
- 2 oz. white grapefruit juice
- 2 oz. mandarin orange juice
- ¾ oz. gin
- ½ oz. Domaine de Canton ginger liqueur

1. In a shaker, muddle the basil leaves.
2. Fill shaker three-fourths full with ice. Add the juices, gin and ginger liqueur; cover and shake until condensation forms on the outside of the shaker, 10-15 seconds. Strain into a chilled cocktail glass.

1 serving: 136 cal., 0 fat (0 sat. fat), 0 chol., 0 sod., 14g carb. (7g sugars, 0 fiber), 1g pro.

CRUNCHY VEGETABLE DIP

This new recipe was a big hit with my family. Dig into it as an appetizer or for a light lunch.
—Dottie Miller, Jonesborough, TN

PREP: 15 MIN. + CHILLING
MAKES: 16 SERVINGS

- 1 pkg. (8 oz.) cream cheese, softened
- 1 Tbsp. mayonnaise
- 1 Tbsp. lemon juice
- ½ tsp. salt
- ⅛ tsp. pepper
- ¾ cup grated carrots
- ½ cup diced celery
- ½ cup diced green pepper
- ⅓ cup chopped green onions
  Assorted crackers and fresh vegetables

In a bowl, beat first 5 ingredients until smooth. Stir in vegetables. Refrigerate, covered, 2-3 hours. Serve with crackers and vegetables.

2 Tbsp. dip: 60 cal., 6g fat (3g sat. fat), 14mg chol., 129mg sod., 2g carb. (1g sugars, 0 fiber), 1g pro.

BLACKBERRY LEMONADE

Here's a special drink that's perfect when blackberries are in season. It has a tangy, refreshing flavor.
—Rich Murray, Nevada, MO

PREP: 20 MIN. + CHILLING
MAKES: ABOUT 1½ QT.

- 4 cups water, divided
- 1 cup sugar
- 1 cup lemon juice
- 1 Tbsp. grated lemon zest
- 1 cup blackberries
- 1 to 2 drops blue food coloring, optional

1. In a large saucepan, bring 2 cups water and sugar to a boil. Boil mixture for 2 minutes, stirring occasionally. Remove from the heat. Stir in lemon juice, zest and the remaining water; cool slightly.
2. In a blender, combine 1 cup of lemon mixture and the blackberries; cover and process until blended. Strain and discard seeds. Pour blackberry mixture and remaining lemon mixture into a pitcher; stir well. Add food coloring if desired. Refrigerate until chilled. Serve in chilled glasses over ice.

1 cup: 152 cal., 0 fat (0 sat. fat), 0 chol., 1mg sod., 40g carb. (35g sugars, 2g fiber), 0 pro.

PEACHY JALAPENO GUACAMOLE

Fresh jalapenos and summer-ripe peaches give this creamy guacamole so much flavor. It's got a little kick, but I love that it's not so spicy that it burns off my taste buds!
—Colleen Delawder, Herndon, VA

TAKES: 15 MIN. • **MAKES:** 1½ CUPS

- 2 medium ripe avocados, peeled and cubed
- 2 Tbsp. lime juice
- ½ tsp. kosher salt
- ½ tsp. ground cumin
- ¼ tsp. pepper
- 1 medium peach, peeled and finely chopped
- 1 jalapeno pepper, seeded and minced
- 2 Tbsp. finely chopped red onion
  Tortilla chips

Mash avocados with lime juice, salt, cumin and pepper. Gently stir in peach, jalapeno and red onion. Serve with tortilla chips.
¼ cup: 90 cal., 7g fat (1g sat. fat), 0 chol., 164mg sod., 7g carb. (2g sugars, 4g fiber), 1g pro. **Diabetic exchanges:** 1 fat, ½ starch.

Leave the seeds in the jalapeno pepper for extra heat.

HONEY HYDRATOR

Stir up a pitcher of this refreshing drink, naturally sweetened with honey.
—National Honey Board, Firestone, CO

TAKES: 5 MIN.
MAKES: 8 SERVINGS

- ½ cup lukewarm water
- ½ cup honey
- ½ tsp. salt substitute or ¼ tsp. salt
- 2 cups cold orange juice
- 5 cups cold water

Place water, honey and salt substitute in a pitcher; stir until blended. Stir in juice and cold water. Refrigerate until serving.
1 cup: 94 cal., 0 fat (0 sat. fat), 0 chol., 76mg sod., 24g carb. (23g sugars, 0 fiber), 0 pro.
Diabetic exchanges: 1½ starch.

SWEET ONION PIMIENTO CHEESE DEVILED EGGS

For my mother's 92nd birthday, we had deviled eggs topped with pimientos as part of the spread. They're timeless and always in good taste.
—Linda Foreman, Locust Grove, OK

TAKES: 15 MIN. • **MAKES:** 1 DOZEN

- 6 hard-boiled large eggs
- ¼ cup finely shredded sharp cheddar cheese
- 2 Tbsp. mayonnaise
- 4 tsp. diced pimientos, drained
- 2 tsp. finely chopped sweet onion
- 1 tsp. Dijon mustard
- 1 small garlic clove, minced
- ¼ tsp. salt
- ⅛ tsp. pepper
  Additional diced pimientos and finely shredded sharp cheddar cheese

Cut eggs lengthwise in half. Remove yolks, reserving whites. In a bowl, mash yolks. Stir in the cheese, mayonnaise, pimientos, onion, mustard, garlic, salt and pepper. Spoon or pipe into the egg whites. Sprinkle with additional diced pimientos and cheese. Refrigerate, covered, until serving.
1 stuffed egg half: 67 cal., 5g fat (2g sat. fat), 96mg chol., 128mg sod., 1g carb. (0 sugars, 0 fiber), 4g pro.

MARGARITA CHICKEN QUESADILLAS

Quesadillas never taste as good as when they are filled with slightly sweet onions and peppers and topped with lime butter and salt, the perfect balance of sweet and savory. This version is a refreshing recipe for a summer party—or a great way to bring a little bit of summer into the cold winter months.

—Stephanie Bright, Simpsonville, SC

PREP: 35 MIN. + MARINATING • **BAKE:** 10 MIN.
MAKES: 16 SERVINGS

- 4 boneless skinless chicken breast halves (5 oz. each)
- ¾ cup thawed frozen limeade concentrate
- 1 large onion, sliced
- 1 medium sweet orange pepper, julienned
- 1 medium sweet yellow pepper, julienned
- 1 Tbsp. canola oil
- ¼ tsp. salt
- ¼ tsp. pepper
- 4 flour tortillas (10 in.)
- 1 cup shredded Monterey Jack cheese
- 1 cup shredded cheddar cheese
- 2 Tbsp. butter, melted
- 1 Tbsp. lime juice
- 1 Tbsp. chopped fresh cilantro
  Lime wedges, optional

1. Place chicken in a large bowl. Add limeade concentrate and toss to coat. Cover bowl; refrigerate at least 6 hours or overnight.
2. In a large nonstick skillet, saute the onion and sweet peppers in oil until tender; season with salt and pepper. Remove and set aside; wipe out skillet. Drain chicken and discard marinade.
3. Grill chicken, covered, on a greased rack over medium heat or broil 4 in. from the heat for 5-8 minutes on each side or until a thermometer reads 170°. Cut chicken into ¼-in. strips; set aside. On 1 half of each tortilla, layer Monterey Jack cheese, chicken, pepper mixture and cheddar cheese; fold over. Combine the butter and lime juice; brush over the tortillas.
4. In the same skillet used to cook the vegetables, cook the quesadillas over medium heat until cheese is melted, 2-3 minutes per side. Keep warm in oven while cooking remaining quesadillas. Cut each quesadilla into 4 wedges. Sprinkle with cilantro; serve with lime wedges if desired.

1 wedge: 204 cal., 9g fat (4g sat. fat), 37mg chol., 288mg sod., 18g carb. (8g sugars, 1g fiber), 12g pro.

HOW MUCH IS ENOUGH?

Whether hosting a backyard bash, bridal shower or family reunion, it's key to have enough appetizers for the crowd. Keep these guidelines in mind when planning your party.

COCKTAILS BEFORE DINNER:
Plan on 3-4 types of appetizers and 4-5 servings per guest.

OPEN HOUSE BUFFET:
Serve 4-5 appetizers and 4-6 servings per person.

LIGHT DINNER OF FINGER FOODS:
Consider offering 6-8 appetizers and estimate 14-16 servings per guest.

SLAW-TOPPED BEEF SLIDERS

When I was working full time, I would rely on these delicious, fast-to-fix beef sliders for simple meals. To cut down prep time and avoid extra cleanup, I used bagged coleslaw mix and bottled slaw dressing.
—Jane Whittaker, Pensacola, FL

PREP: 20 MIN. • **COOK:** 6 HOURS.
MAKES: 1 DOZEN

- 3 cups coleslaw mix
- ½ medium red onion, chopped (about ⅔ cup)
- ⅛ tsp. celery seed
- ¼ tsp. pepper
- ⅓ cup coleslaw salad dressing

SANDWICHES
- 1 boneless beef chuck roast (2 lbs.)
- 1 tsp. salt
- ½ tsp. pepper
- 1 can (6 oz.) tomato paste
- ¼ cup water
- 1 tsp. Worcestershire sauce
- 1 small onion, diced
- 1 cup barbecue sauce
- 12 slider buns or dinner rolls, split

1. Combine coleslaw, onion, celery seed and pepper. Add salad dressing; toss to coat. Refrigerate until serving.
2. Sprinkle roast with salt and pepper; transfer roast to a 5-qt. slow cooker. Mix tomato paste, water and Worcestershire sauce; pour over roast. Top with onion. Cook, covered, on low 6-8 hours or until meat is tender.
3. Shred meat with 2 forks; return to the slow cooker. Stir in barbecue sauce; heat through. Serve beef on buns; top with coleslaw. Replace tops.
1 slider: 322 cal., 12g fat (4g sat. fat), 67mg chol., 726mg sod., 34g carb. (13g sugars, 3g fiber), 20g pro.

SLAW-TOPPED BEEF SLIDERS

HOT DOG SLIDERS WITH MANGO-PINEAPPLE SALSA

For parties, we shrink down lots of foods to slider size, including these quick hot dogs. Pile on the easy—but irresistible—fruit salsa for a burst of fresh flavor.
—Carole Resnick, Cleveland, OH

TAKES: 30 MIN.
MAKES: 2 DOZEN (2 CUPS SALSA)

- 3 Tbsp. lime juice
- 2 Tbsp. honey
- ¼ tsp. salt
- 1 cup cubed fresh pineapple (½ in.)
- 1 cup cubed peeled mango (½ in.)
- ¼ cup finely chopped red onion
- 2 Tbsp. finely chopped sweet red pepper
- 12 hot dogs
- 12 hot dog buns, split

1. In a small bowl, whisk lime juice, honey and salt until blended. Add pineapple, mango, onion and pepper; toss to coat.
2. Grill the hot dogs, covered, over medium heat or broil 4 in. from heat until heated through, 7-9 minutes, turning occasionally.
3. Place hot dogs in buns; cut each crosswise in half. Serve with fruit salsa.
1 slider with 1 Tbsp. salsa: 146 cal., 8g fat (3g sat. fat), 13mg chol., 361mg sod., 15g carb. (5g sugars, 1g fiber), 5g pro.

MARINATED MOZZARELLA & TOMATO APPETIZERS

MARINATED MOZZARELLA & TOMATO APPETIZERS

This party hit was inspired by a dish I ate at a restaurant. It's best served chilled and should marinate for a few days—the longer the better. My daughter likes to put the mozzarella on her antipasti platters.
—Mary Ann Lee, Clifton Park, NY

PREP: 15 MIN. + MARINATING • **BAKE:** 5 MIN.
MAKES: 16 SERVINGS

- ½ cup Italian salad dressing
- 2 Tbsp. minced fresh basil
- 2 Tbsp. minced fresh chives
- ½ tsp. coarsely ground pepper
- 2 cartons (8 oz. each) miniature fresh mozzarella cheese balls, drained
- 2 cups cherry tomatoes
- 12 slices French bread baguette (½ in. thick), cut into quarters
- 2 tsp. olive oil
- ⅛ tsp. salt

1. Preheat oven to 450°. Combine salad dressing, basil, chives and pepper. Add the cheese and tomatoes; toss to coat. Refrigerate, covered, at least 3 hours to let flavors blend.
2. Meanwhile, toss baguette pieces with oil and salt; arrange on a baking sheet. Bake until toasted, 4-5 minutes. Cool completely. Just before serving, add toasted bread to cheese mixture; toss to combine. If desired, thread tomatoes, cheese and bread on skewers.
¼ cup: 119 cal., 8g fat (4g sat. fat), 22mg chol., 171mg sod., 5g carb. (2g sugars, 0 fiber), 6g pro.

SWEET GINGERED
CHICKEN WINGS

STRAWBERRY MELON FIZZ

Experimenting in the kitchen is fun for me. I came up with this by combining two recipes—one for a melon ball basket and one for a sparkling beverage.
—Teresa Messick, Montgomery, AL

TAKES: 30 MIN. • **MAKES:** 10 SERVINGS

    2 cups sugar
    1 cup water
    5 fresh mint sprigs
    1 qt. fresh strawberries, halved
    2 cups cubed honeydew
 1¾ cups cubed cantaloupe
       Ginger ale or sparkling white
       grape juice

1. In a large saucepan, combine the sugar, water and mint; bring to a boil. Reduce the heat; simmer 10 minutes. Remove from the heat; allow to cool completely. Discard mint.
2. Combine strawberries and melon. Just before serving, fill tall glasses with fruit and drizzle each with 1 Tbsp. syrup. Add ginger ale to each glass.
1 serving: 194 cal., 0 fat (0 sat. fat), 0 chol., 7mg sod., 49g carb. (46g sugars, 2g fiber), 1g pro.

SWEET GINGERED CHICKEN WINGS

When I prepare this recipe for a get-together, it's one of the first dishes to disappear. I first tasted the delicious chicken wings 11 years ago when I attended a class on using honey in cooking. Now I even use this recipe for a main course.
—Debbie Dougal, Roseville, CA

PREP: 10 MIN. • **BAKE:** 1 HOUR
MAKES: 2 DOZEN

    1 cup all-purpose flour
    2 tsp. salt
    2 tsp. paprika
   ¼ tsp. pepper
   24 chicken wings (about 5 lbs.)
SAUCE
   ¼ cup honey
   ¼ cup thawed orange juice
       concentrate
   ½ tsp. ground ginger
       Minced fresh parsley, optional

1. Preheat oven to 350°. Line 2 baking sheets with foil; coat with cooking spray.
2. In a shallow dish, combine flour, salt, paprika and pepper. Add chicken wings, a few at a time; toss to coat. Divide the wings between prepared pans. Bake 30 minutes.
3. In a small bowl, combine honey, orange juice concentrate and ginger; brush over chicken wings. Bake until juices run clear, 25-30 minutes.
4. Preheat broiler. Broil wings 4 in. from heat until lightly browned, 1-2 minutes. If desired, sprinkle with parsley.
1 chicken wing: 134 cal., 7g fat (2g sat. fat), 29mg chol., 225mg sod., 8g carb. (4g sugars, 0 fiber), 10g pro.

SUMMER'S TOP

SALADS & DRESSINGS

Memorable summer menus aren't complete without garden-fresh sidekicks that complement any entree. See how easy it is to toss together a hit that rounds out any warm-weather meal.

POTLUCK ANTIPASTO
PASTA SALAD

POTLUCK ANTIPASTO PASTA SALAD

I love trying new recipes, and this one for pasta salad tops all other varieties I've tried. With beans, cheese, sausage and vegetables, it's a hearty complement to any meal.
—Bernadette Nelson, Arcadia, CA

TAKES: 30 MIN. • **MAKES:** 18 SERVINGS

- 1 pkg. (16 oz.) penne pasta
- 1 can (15 oz.) garbanzo beans or chickpeas, rinsed and drained
- 1 medium sweet red or green pepper, julienned
- 2 plum tomatoes, halved lengthwise and sliced
- 1 bunch green onions, sliced
- 4 oz. Monterey Jack cheese, julienned
- 4 oz. part-skim mozzarella cheese, julienned
- 4 oz. brick or provolone cheese, julienned
- 4 oz. thinly sliced hard salami, julienned
- 3 oz. thinly sliced pepperoni
- 1 can (2¼ oz.) sliced ripe olives, drained
- 1 to 2 Tbsp. minced chives

BASIL VINAIGRETTE

- ⅔ cup canola oil
- ⅓ cup red wine vinegar
- 3 Tbsp. minced fresh basil or 1 Tbsp. dried basil
- 1 garlic clove, minced
- ¼ tsp. salt

1. Cook pasta according to package directions; rinse with cold water and drain. In a large bowl, combine pasta, garbanzo beans, vegetables, cheeses, meats, olives and chives.
2. In a small bowl, whisk the vinaigrette ingredients. Pour over the salad; toss to coat. Cover and refrigerate. Toss salad before serving.

1 cup: 248 cal., 18g fat (5g sat. fat), 24mg chol., 431mg sod., 13g carb. (2g sugars, 2g fiber), 9g pro.

To keep pasta from sticking together while cooking, use a large pot with plenty of water.

STRAWBERRY SALAD WITH POPPY SEED DRESSING

STRAWBERRY SALAD WITH POPPY SEED DRESSING

My family is always happy to see this fruit and veggie salad. If strawberries aren't available, substitute mandarin oranges and dried cranberries.
—Irene Keller, Kalamazoo, MI

TAKES: 30 MIN. • **MAKES:** 10 SERVINGS

- ¼ cup sugar
- ⅓ cup slivered almonds
- 1 bunch romaine, torn (about 8 cups)
- 1 small onion, halved and thinly sliced
- 2 cups halved fresh strawberries

DRESSING

- ¼ cup mayonnaise
- 2 Tbsp. sugar
- 1 Tbsp. sour cream
- 1 Tbsp. 2% milk
- 2¼ tsp. cider vinegar
- 1½ tsp. poppy seeds

1. Place sugar in a small heavy skillet; cook and stir over medium-low heat until melted and caramel-colored, about 10 minutes. Stir in almonds until coated. Spread on foil to cool.
2. Place the romaine, onion and strawberries in a large bowl. Whisk together dressing ingredients; toss with salad. Break candied almonds into pieces; sprinkle over the salad. Serve immediately.

¾ cup: 110 cal., 6g fat (1g sat. fat), 1mg chol., 33mg sod., 13g carb. (10g sugars, 2g fiber), 2g pro. **Diabetic exchanges:** 1 vegetable, 1 fat, ½ starch.

Turn this fresh fruit salad into something heartier. Grill 2 pounds boneless skinless chicken breasts, slice and add to the salad for an easy main dish.

BASIC BUTTERMILK SALAD DRESSING

This easy recipe comes in handy when I'm serving salad to a crowd,. It makes a full quart of creamy, delicious dressing to toss with favorite greens and veggies.

—Patricia Mele, Lower Burrell, PA

TAKES: 5 MIN. • **MAKES:** 32 SERVINGS (1 QT.)

- 2 cups mayonnaise
- 2 cups buttermilk
- 1 Tbsp. onion powder
- 1 Tbsp. dried parsley flakes
- 1½ tsp. garlic powder
- ½ tsp. salt
- ½ tsp. celery salt
- ¼ tsp. pepper

Whisk together all ingredients. Refrigerate, covered, until serving.

2 Tbsp.: 98 cal., 10g fat (2g sat. fat), 2mg chol., 155mg sod., 1g carb. (1g sugars, 0 fiber), 1g pro. **Diabetic exchanges:** 2 fat.

TOMATO AVOCADO & GRILLED CORN SALAD

TOMATO AVOCADO & GRILLED CORN SALAD

With ripe tomatoes, fresh basil and grilled corn off the cob, this sunny salad tastes just like summertime!

—Angela Spengler, Niceville, FL

PREP: 20 MIN. • **GRILL:** 10 MIN. + COOLING
MAKES: 8 SERVINGS

- 1 medium ear sweet corn, husks removed
- 3 large red tomatoes, sliced
- 3 large yellow tomatoes, sliced
- ¾ tsp. kosher salt, divided
- ½ tsp. pepper, divided
- 2 medium ripe avocados, peeled and sliced
- ¼ cup olive oil
- 2 Tbsp. red wine vinegar
- 1 Tbsp. minced fresh basil, plus more for garnish
- ⅓ cup crumbled feta cheese

1. Grill corn, covered, over medium heat 10-12 minutes or until lightly browned and tender, turning occasionally. Cool slightly. Cut corn from cob.

2. Arrange tomato on large serving platter. Sprinkle with ½ tsp. salt and ¼ tsp. pepper. Top with avocado slices. Whisk together the oil, vinegar, basil and the remaining salt and pepper; drizzle half over the tomatoes and avocado. Top with grilled corn and feta; drizzle remaining dressing over top. Garnish with additional chopped basil.

1 serving: 164 cal., 13g fat (2g sat. fat), 3mg chol., 237mg sod., 11g carb. (4g sugars, 4g fiber), 3g pro. **Diabetic exchanges:** 2 fat, 1 vegetable, ½ starch.

This dish is spectacular with fresh heirloom tomatoes, and all that flavor means you can use less salt.

KHMER PICKLED
VEGETABLE SALAD

KHMER PICKLED
VEGETABLE SALAD

I grew up as a missionary kid in Cambodia, and now most of my favorite foods have a Southeast Asian background. Many locals love eating this pickled salad for breakfast, but I like it for lunch with satay chicken.
—Hannah Heavener, Belton, TX

PREP: 25 MIN. + CHILLING
COOK: 5 MIN.
MAKES: 16 SERVINGS

- 2 medium daikon radishes (about 1¼ lbs. each), peeled and thinly sliced
- 4 cups shredded cabbage (about ½ small)
- 1 large cucumber, thinly sliced
- 2 medium carrots, thinly sliced
- 1 cup cut fresh green beans (2 in.)
- ½ medium red onion, thinly sliced
- 1 piece fresh gingerroot (1 in.), thinly sliced
- 2 Thai chili or serrano peppers, halved lengthwise and seeded if desired
- 2 cups rice vinegar
- ¾ cup sugar
- 2 tsp. salt
- 2 Tbsp. chopped fresh cilantro

1. Place first 8 ingredients in a large nonreactive bowl. Place the vinegar, sugar and salt in a 2-cup or larger glass measuring cup; microwave until warm, 2-3 minutes. Stir until sugar is dissolved. Stir into the vegetables. Refrigerate, covered, at least 1 hour before serving.
2. To serve, sprinkle with cilantro. Serve with a slotted spoon.
¾ cup: 99 cal., 0 fat (0 sat. fat), 0 chol., 794mg sod., 25g carb. (22g sugars, 2g fiber), 1g pro.

WARM GREEN BEAN
& POTATO SALAD

The combination of green beans and red potatoes, sometimes called "green beans Pierre," is one of my go-to side dishes. It's terrific with chicken.
—Preci D'Silva, Dubai, AA

TAKES: 30 MIN. • **MAKES:** 10 SERVINGS

- 1 lb. small red potatoes, quartered
- ¼ cup olive oil
- 2 Tbsp. white wine vinegar
- ½ tsp. salt
- ⅛ tsp. each garlic powder, ground mustard and pepper
- ⅛ tsp. each dried basil, parsley flakes and tarragon
- 1 lb. fresh green beans, cut into 2-in. pieces
- 2 medium tomatoes, coarsely chopped
- 2 Tbsp. chopped onion

1. Place potatoes in a large saucepan; add water to cover. Bring to a boil. Cook, uncovered, for 10 minutes. Meanwhile, in a large bowl, whisk the oil, vinegar and seasonings.
2. Add green beans to potatoes; return to a boil. Cook 3-5 minutes longer or until the vegetables are tender. Drain; add to the dressing and toss to coat. Stir in the tomatoes and onion. Serve warm.
¾ cup: 100 cal., 5g fat (1g sat. fat), 0 chol., 125mg sod., 12g carb. (2g sugars, 3g fiber), 2g pro. **Diabetic exchanges:** 1 vegetable, ½ starch.

CAESAR DRESSING

Looking for a new and different salad dressing you can whisk up in minutes for special occasions? You can't miss with this light, savory Caesar blend from our Test Kitchen. It really dresses up fresh greens!
—*Taste of Home* Test Kitchen

PREP: 15 MIN. + CHILLING • **MAKES:** 1⅔ CUPS

- ⅔ cup reduced-fat mayonnaise
- ½ cup reduced-fat sour cream
- ½ cup buttermilk
- 1 Tbsp. red wine vinegar
- 1 Tbsp. stone-ground mustard
- 1½ tsp. lemon juice
- 1½ tsp. Worcestershire sauce
- ⅓ cup grated Parmigiano-Reggiano cheese
- 2 anchovy fillets, minced
- 2 garlic cloves, minced
- ½ tsp. coarsely ground pepper

In a small bowl, whisk mayonnaise, sour cream, buttermilk, vinegar, mustard, lemon juice and Worcestershire sauce. Stir in cheese, anchovies, garlic and pepper. Cover and refrigerate at least 1 hour.
2 Tbsp.: 71 cal., 6g fat (2g sat. fat), 10mg chol., 205mg sod., 3g carb. (2g sugars, 0 fiber), 2g pro. **Diabetic exchanges:** 1 fat.

KANSAS CUCUMBER SALAD

Cucumbers are my very favorite garden vegetable, so I use this recipe often. I got it from a friend eight years ago. I've heard this refreshing dish keeps very well in the refrigerator, but it goes so fast around our house, I've never found out for myself.
—Karen Ann Bland, Gove City, KS

PREP: 10 MIN. + CHILLING
MAKES: 8 SERVINGS

- 1 cup Miracle Whip
- ¼ cup sugar
- 4 tsp. cider vinegar
- ½ tsp. dill weed
- ½ tsp. salt, optional
- 4 medium cucumbers, peeled and thinly sliced
- 3 green onions, chopped

In a large bowl, combine Miracle Whip, sugar, vinegar, dill and, if desired, salt; mix well. Add cucumbers and onions; toss. Cover and chill for at least 1 hour.
⅔ cup: 122 cal., 7g fat (1g sat. fat), 2mg chol., 201mg sod., 12g carb. (10g sugars, 2g fiber), 2g pro.

GARDEN BOUNTY PANZANELLA SALAD

When my sister gave me fresh tomatoes and basil, I made this traditional bread salad. The longer it sits, the more the bread soaks up the seasonings.
—Jannine Fisk, Malden, MA

PREP: 15 MIN. • **COOK:** 20 MIN.
MAKES: 16 SERVINGS

- ¼ cup olive oil
- 12 oz. French or ciabatta bread, cut into 1-in. cubes (about 12 cups)
- 4 large tomatoes, coarsely chopped
- 1 English cucumber, coarsely chopped
- 1 medium green pepper, cut into 1-in. pieces
- 1 medium sweet yellow pepper, cut into 1-in. pieces
- 1 small red onion, halved and thinly sliced
- ½ cup coarsely chopped fresh basil
- ¼ cup grated Parmesan cheese
- ¾ tsp. kosher salt
- ¼ tsp. coarsely ground pepper
- ½ cup Italian salad dressing

1. In a large skillet, heat 2 Tbsp. oil over medium heat. Add half of the bread cubes; cook and stir until toasted, about 8 minutes. Remove from pan. Repeat with remaining oil and bread cubes.
2. Combine the bread cubes, tomatoes, cucumber, peppers, onion, basil, cheese, salt and pepper. Toss with dressing.
1 cup: 131 cal., 6g fat (1g sat. fat), 1mg chol., 310mg sod., 18g carb. (3g sugars, 2g fiber), 3g pro. **Diabetic exchanges:** 1 starch, 1 vegetable, 1 fat.

RED, WHITE & BLUE SUMMER SALAD

Caprese and fresh fruit always remind me of summer. In this salad, I combined traditional Caprese flavors with summer blueberries and peaches, and added prosciutto for saltiness, creating a balanced and flavor-packed popular side dish.
—Emily Falke, Santa Barbara, CA

TAKES: 25 MIN. • **MAKES:** 12 SERVINGS

- ⅔ cup extra virgin olive oil
- ½ cup julienned fresh basil
- ⅓ cup white balsamic vinegar
- ¼ cup julienned fresh mint leaves
- 2 garlic cloves, minced
- 2 tsp. Dijon mustard
- 1 tsp. sea salt
- 1 tsp. sugar
- 1 tsp. pepper
- 2 cups cherry tomatoes
- 8 cups fresh arugula
- 1 carton (8 oz.) fresh mozzarella cheese pearls, drained
- 2 medium peaches, sliced
- 2 cups fresh blueberries
- 6 oz. thinly sliced prosciutto, julienned

1. In a small bowl, whisk the first 9 ingredients. Add tomatoes; let stand while preparing the salad.
2. In a large bowl, combine arugula, mozzarella, peach slices, blueberries, and prosciutto. Pour tomato mixture over top; toss to coat. Garnish with additional mint leaves. Serve the salad immediately.
1 cup: 233 cal., 18g fat (5g sat. fat), 27mg chol., 486mg sod., 10g carb. (8g sugars, 2g fiber), 8g pro.

MAMA'S WARM GERMAN POTATO SALAD

My grandmother, Mama, made this potato salad for every family gathering held at her home. Each relative would come with their specialties in hand. She never wrote the recipe down, so I had to re-create it from memory. Years later, it's just about right.
—Charlene Chambers, Ormond Beach, FL

PREP: 20 MIN. • **COOK:** 30 MIN.
MAKES: 12 SERVINGS

- 3 lbs. small red potatoes
- ⅓ cup canola oil
- 2 Tbsp. champagne vinegar
- 1 tsp. kosher salt
- ½ tsp. coarsely ground pepper
- ½ English cucumber, very thinly sliced
- 2 celery ribs, thinly sliced
- 1 small onion, chopped
- 6 bacon strips, cooked and crumbled
- 1 Tbsp. minced fresh parsley

Place potatoes in a large saucepan; add water to cover. Bring to a boil. Reduce the heat; cook, uncovered, until tender, 18-21 minutes. Drain; cool slightly. Peel and thinly slice. Whisk oil, vinegar, salt and pepper. Add potatoes; toss to coat. Add remaining ingredients; toss to combine. Serve warm.
¾ cup: 163 cal., 8g fat (1g sat. fat), 4mg chol., 246mg sod., 20g carb. (2g sugars, 2g fiber), 4g pro. **Diabetic exchanges:** 1½ fat, 1 starch.

LEMON VINAIGRETTE

Add a spark of citrus to your salads with this quick and easy vinaigrette. Try it over a fresh spinach salad or use it to jazz up a side dish of roasted veggies.
—Sarah Farmer, Waukesha, WI

PREP: 5 MIN. • **MAKES:** ½ CUP

- 2 Tbsp. fresh lemon juice
- 2 tsp. Dijon mustard
- ¼ tsp. salt
- ⅛ tsp. coarsely ground pepper
- 6 Tbsp. extra virgin olive oil

In a large bowl, whisk together the first 4 ingredients. Slowly add olive oil while whisking constantly.
2 Tbsp.: 183 cal., 20g fat (3g sat. fat), 0 chol., 208mg sod., 1g carb. (0 sugars, 0 fiber), 0 pro.

For the best results, start with all the ingredients at room temperature. If the oil is cool or cold, it is much more difficult to form the emulsion.

SUMMER'S RIPEST

FRUITS & BERRIES

Few foods represent summer like ripe, juicy fruits and berries. This section shows how easily the season's freshest produce dresses up everything from sweet sensations to savory entrees.

ONE-POT SALSA CHICKEN

This tasty recipe is a colorful and healthy main dish that can be on the table in just over an hour. The subtle sweet-spicy flavor is a nice surprise.
—Ann Sheehy, Lawrence, MA

PREP: 20 MIN. • **COOK:** 45 MIN.
MAKES: 6 SERVINGS

- 2   Tbsp. canola oil
- 2   lbs. boneless skinless chicken thighs, cut into 1-in. pieces
- 1   tsp. pepper
- ½   tsp. salt
- 2   medium sweet potatoes, peeled and chopped
- 1   jar (16 oz.) medium salsa
- 2   medium nectarines, peeled and chopped
- 2   Tbsp. Tajin seasoning
- 1   cup uncooked instant brown rice
- 1   cup water
- ¼   cup minced fresh parsley
      Minced fresh chives

1. In a Dutch oven, heat oil over medium-high heat. Sprinkle chicken with pepper and salt. Brown the chicken in batches; return to pan. Add the sweet potatoes, salsa, nectarines and seasoning. Bring to a boil; reduce heat. Cover and simmer until potatoes are almost tender, about 15 minutes.
2. Stir in rice and water; bring to a boil. Reduce heat. Cover and simmer until potatoes are tender, about 10 minutes. Stir in parsley. Serve in bowls; sprinkle with chives.
1⅔ cups: 432 cal., 16g fat (3g sat. fat), 101mg chol., 1254mg sod., 39g carb. (13g sugars, 4g fiber), 31g pro.

SPICY PLUM SALMON

5i SPICY PLUM SALMON

I created this sweet and spicy salmon after being challenged to use healthier ingredients. The fresh plum sauce really complements the smoky grilled fish.
—Cheryl Hochstettler, Richmond, TX

PREP: 25 MIN. • **GRILL:** 10 MIN.
MAKES: 6 SERVINGS

- 5   medium plums, divided
- ½   cup water
- 2   Tbsp. ketchup
- 1   chipotle pepper in adobo sauce, finely chopped
- 1   Tbsp. sugar
- 1   Tbsp. olive oil
- 6   salmon fillets (6 oz. each)
- ¾   tsp. salt

1. Coarsely chop 2 plums; place in a small saucepan. Add water; bring to a boil. Reduce heat; simmer, uncovered, 10-15 minutes or until the plums are softened and the liquid is almost evaporated. Cool slightly. Transfer to a food processor; add ketchup, chipotle, sugar and oil. Process until pureed. Reserve ¾ cup sauce for serving.
2. Sprinkle salmon with salt; place on a greased grill rack, skin side up. Grill, covered, over medium heat until fish just begins to flake easily with a fork, about 10 minutes. Brush with remaining sauce during last 3 minutes. Slice remaining plums. Serve salmon with plum slices and reserved sauce.
1 fillet with ½ plum and 2 Tbsp. sauce: 325 cal., 18g fat (3g sat. fat), 85mg chol., 460mg sod., 10g carb. (9g sugars, 1g fiber), 29g pro. **Diabetic exchanges:** 5 lean meat, 1 fruit, ½ fat.

Plums are a good source of vitamins C, K and A. They're usually small, so try 2 for a healthy snack.

GRANDMA'S OLD-FASHIONED STRAWBERRY SHORTCAKE

GRANDMA'S OLD-FASHIONED STRAWBERRY SHORTCAKE

When my grandma served this shortcake, she usually topped it with homemade vanilla ice cream.

—Angela Lively, Conroe, TX

PREP: 30 MIN. + STANDING • **BAKE:** 20 MIN.
MAKES: 8 SERVINGS

- 6 cups sliced fresh strawberries
- ½ cup sugar
- 1 tsp. vanilla extract

SHORTCAKE
- 3 cups all-purpose flour
- 5 Tbsp. sugar, divided
- 3 tsp. baking powder
- 1 tsp. baking soda
- ½ tsp. salt
- ¾ cup cold butter, cubed
- 1¼ cups buttermilk
- 2 Tbsp. heavy whipping cream

TOPPING
- 1½ cups heavy whipping cream
- 2 Tbsp. sugar
- ½ tsp. vanilla extract

1. Combine strawberries with sugar and vanilla; mash slightly. Let stand at least 30 minutes, tossing occasionally.
2. Preheat oven to 400°. For shortcake, whisk together the flour, 4 Tbsp. sugar, baking powder, baking soda and salt. Cut in butter until crumbly. Add buttermilk; stir just until combined (do not overmix). Drop batter by ⅓ cupfuls 2 in. apart onto an ungreased baking sheet. Brush with 2 Tbsp. heavy cream; sprinkle with the remaining 1 Tbsp. sugar. Bake until golden, 18-20 minutes. Remove to wire racks to cool completely.
3. For topping, beat heavy whipping cream until it begins to thicken. Add sugar and vanilla; beat until soft peaks form. To serve, cut biscuits in half; top with strawberries and whipped cream.

1 shortcake with ½ cup strawberries and ⅓ cup whipped cream: 638 cal., 36g fat (22g sat. fat), 102mg chol., 710mg sod., 72g carb. (33g sugars, 4g fiber), 9g pro.

PERFECT PLUM & PEACH PIE

I created this recipe to fit with in-season summer fruit. The plums give the pie a splash of color as well as flavor, and the crumb topping is both easy and excellent!
—Rachel Johnson, Shippensburg, PA

PREP: 25 MIN. • **BAKE:** 40 MIN. + COOLING
MAKES: 8 SERVINGS

  1   sheet refrigerated pie crust
FILLING
  6   medium peaches, peeled and sliced
  6   medium black plums, sliced
  ½   cup all-purpose flour
  ½   cup confectioners' sugar
  ½   tsp. ground cinnamon
  ½   tsp. ground nutmeg
TOPPING
  ¼   cup all-purpose flour
  ¼   cup packed brown sugar
  2   Tbsp. butter, softened
  ¼   tsp. ground cinnamon

1. Preheat oven to 375°. Unroll the crust onto a lightly floured surface; roll to a 12-in. circle. Transfer to a 9-in. deep-dish pie plate; trim and flute edge. Refrigerate while preparing filling.
2. Toss peaches and plums with flour, sugar and spices; transfer to crust. Using a fork, mix topping ingredients until crumbly; sprinkle over fruit.
3. Bake on a lower oven rack until golden brown and bubbly, 40-50 minutes. Cool on a wire rack.
1 piece: 311 cal., 10g fat (5g sat. fat), 13mg chol., 125mg sod., 53g carb. (29g sugars, 3g fiber), 4g pro.

MINTED FRUIT SALAD

Filled with the season's best and freshest fruit, this salad shouts summer. The hint of mint adds a refreshing note to the sweet fruit combo.
—Edie DeSpain, Logan, UT

PREP: 20 MIN. + COOLING
MAKES: 6 SERVINGS

  1   cup unsweetened apple juice
  2   Tbsp. honey
  4   tsp. finely chopped crystallized ginger
  4   tsp. lemon juice
  4   cups cantaloupe balls
  1   cup sliced fresh strawberries
  1   cup fresh blueberries
  2   tsp. chopped fresh mint leaves

1. In a small saucepan, combine the apple juice, honey, ginger and lemon juice. Bring to a boil over medium-high heat. Cook and stir for 2 minutes or until mixture is reduced to ¾ cup. Remove from the heat. Cool.
2. In a serving bowl, combine the cantaloupe, strawberries, blueberries and mint. Drizzle with cooled apple juice mixture; gently toss to coat.
1 cup: 113 cal., 1g fat (0 sat. fat), 0 chol., 14mg sod., 28g carb. (23g sugars, 2g fiber), 1g pro. **Diabetic exchanges:** 1 fruit, ½ starch.

🕐 GRILLED HALIBUT WITH BLUEBERRY SALSA

Give halibut a new, summery spin. The salsa may seem sophisticated, but it's really a cinch to prepare.
—Donna Goutermont, Sequim, WA

TAKES: 30 MIN. • **MAKES:** 6 SERVINGS

  2   cups fresh blueberries, divided
  1   small red onion, chopped
  ¼   cup minced fresh cilantro
  1   jalapeno pepper, seeded and chopped
  2   Tbsp. orange juice
  1   Tbsp. balsamic vinegar
  1   tsp. plus 2 Tbsp. olive oil, divided
  ⅛   tsp. plus 1 tsp. salt, divided
  ⅛   tsp. pepper
  6   halibut fillets (5 oz. each)

1. In a small bowl, coarsely mash 1 cup blueberries. Stir in the onion, cilantro, jalapeno, orange juice, vinegar, 1 tsp. oil, ⅛ tsp. salt, pepper and the remaining blueberries. Cover and chill until serving.
2. Meanwhile, drizzle the fillets with remaining oil; sprinkle with remaining salt. Grill halibut, covered, over medium heat for 4-5 minutes on each side or until fish flakes easily with a fork. Serve with blueberry salsa.
Note: Wear disposable gloves when cutting hot peppers; the oils can burn skin. Avoid touching your face.
1 fillet with ⅓ cup salsa: 239 cal., 9g fat (1g sat. fat), 45mg chol., 521mg sod., 9g carb. (6g sugars, 1g fiber), 30g pro. **Diabetic exchanges:** 4 lean meat, 1 fat, ½ starch.

GOLDEN BEET & PEACH SOUP

We had a bumper crop of peaches from our two trees this summer and I've been having fun experimenting with different recipes. After finding a beet soup recipe, I changed it up a bit to include our homegrown golden beets and to suit our tastes.
—Sue Gronholz, Beaver Dam, WI

PREP: 20 MIN. • **BAKE:** 40 MIN. + CHILLING
MAKES: 6 SERVINGS

- 2 lbs. fresh golden beets, peeled and cut into 1-in. cubes
- 1 Tbsp. olive oil
- 2 cups white grape peach juice
- 2 Tbsp. cider vinegar
- ¼ cup plain Greek yogurt
- ¼ tsp. finely chopped fresh tarragon
- 2 medium fresh peaches, peeled and diced
  Additional fresh tarragon sprigs

1. Preheat oven to 400°. Place beets in a 15x10x1-in. baking pan. Drizzle with oil; toss to coat. Roast beets until tender, 40-45 minutes. Cool slightly.
2. Transfer beets to a blender or food processor. Add the juice and vinegar; process until smooth. Refrigerate at least 1 hour. In a small bowl, combine Greek yogurt and tarragon; refrigerate.
3. To serve, divide beet mixture among individual bowls; place a spoonful of yogurt mixture into each bowl. Top with diced peaches and additional tarragon.
⅔ cup: 159 cal., 4g fat (1g sat. fat), 3mg chol., 129mg sod., 31g carb. (26g sugars, 4g fiber), 3g pro. **Diabetic exchanges:** 2 vegetable, 1 fruit, ½ fat.

MANDARIN-BERRY STEAK SALAD

It's hard to believe this satisfying entree salad comes together so quickly. We love it with sirloin steak, but you can try it with cooked chicken breasts or even pork. You'll also want to whisk together the vinaigrette for salads all summer long.
—*Taste of Home* Test Kitchen

TAKES: 25 MIN.
MAKES: 4 SERVINGS (1 CUP VINAIGRETTE)

- 3 Tbsp. olive oil
- ¼ cup cider vinegar
- ¼ cup orange juice
- 2 Tbsp. minced fresh parsley
- 2 Tbsp. honey
- 1 garlic clove, minced
- 1 tsp. chili sauce
- ½ tsp. salt
- 8 cups torn romaine
- ½ lb. cooked sirloin steak, sliced
- 3 cups sliced fresh strawberries
- 1 small red onion, sliced
- 1 can (11 oz.) mandarin oranges, drained
- ½ cup chopped pecans toasted
- 2 oz. fresh goat cheese, crumbled

In a small bowl, whisk the first 8 ingredients; set aside. Divide romaine among 4 plates; top with steak, strawberries, onion, oranges, pecans and cheese. Serve with vinaigrette.
1 serving: 926 calories, 69g fat (12g saturated fat), 118mg cholesterol, 549mg sodium, 39g carbohydrate (28g sugars, 8g fiber), 45g protein.

HOMEMADE STRAWBERRY ICE CREAM

What could be better than a tub of luscious homemade ice cream made with fresh strawberries? Having an ice cream social at church with more of the same!
—Esther Johnson, Merrill, WI

PREP: 20 MIN. + COOLING
PROCESS: 20 MIN./BATCH + FREEZING
MAKES: 12 SERVINGS (ABOUT 1½ QT.)

- 6 large egg yolks
- 2 cups whole milk
- 1 cup sugar
- ¼ tsp. salt
- 1 tsp. vanilla extract
- 2 cups heavy whipping cream
- 2 cups crushed fresh strawberries, sweetened

1. Place egg yolks and milk in the top of a double boiler; beat. Add sugar and salt. Cook over simmering water, stirring until mixture is thickened and coats a metal spoon. Cool.
2. Add vanilla, cream and strawberries. Pour into the cylinder of an ice cream freezer and freeze according to the manufacturer's directions. When the ice cream is frozen, transfer mixture to a freezer container; freeze for 2-4 hours before serving.
½ cup: 265 cal., 19g fat (11g sat. fat), 166mg chol., 88mg sod., 22g carb. (21g sugars, 1g fiber), 4g pro.

JALAPENO CORNBREAD FILLED WITH BLUEBERRY QUICK JAM

Fresh jalapenos and blueberry quick jam make the perfect blend of sweet and spicy in this unusual cornbread. Once you eat one piece, you won't be able to resist going back for another.
—Colleen Delawder, Herndon, VA

PREP: 20 MIN. + CHILLING
BAKE: 30 MIN. + COOLING
MAKES: 12 SERVINGS

- 2 cups fresh blueberries
- 1 cup sugar
- 1 Tbsp. cider vinegar
- ¼ tsp. kosher salt

CORNBREAD
- ½ cup 2% milk
- 1 Tbsp. lemon juice
- 1½ cups all-purpose flour
- ½ cup yellow cornmeal
- ½ cup sugar
- 3 tsp. baking powder
- ½ tsp. kosher salt
- 2 Tbsp. unsalted butter
- 1 Tbsp. honey
- 2 large eggs, room temperature
- ⅓ cup canola oil
- 2 jalapeno peppers, seeded and minced

1. In a large heavy saucepan, combine blueberries, sugar, vinegar and kosher salt. Bring to a boil over high heat. Cook, stirring constantly, 5 minutes. Cool mixture completely. Refrigerate, covered, overnight.

2. For cornbread, preheat oven to 350°. Combine milk and lemon juice; let stand briefly. In another bowl, whisk the next 5 ingredients. In a bowl, microwave the butter and honey on high for 30 seconds; cool slightly. Whisk eggs and oil into milk mixture (the mixture may look curdled). Add the butter mixture; whisk until well combined. Add flour mixture; whisk just until combined. Fold in the jalapenos.

3. Pour 2 cups batter into a well-buttered 10-in. fluted tube pan. Spoon half to three-fourths of the blueberry quick jam on top. Cover with remaining batter. Bake until a toothpick inserted in center comes out clean, 30-35 minutes. Cool 10 minutes; invert onto a cake plate or serving platter. Drizzle with remaining blueberry quick jam.

1 piece: 289 cal., 10g fat (2g sat. fat), 37mg chol., 258mg sod., 48g carb. (30g sugars, 1g fiber), 4g pro.

BERRY WHITE ICE POPS

Kids and adults alike will love these ice pops. Speckled with colorful mixed berries, they make for a cool fruity treat.
—Sharon Guinta, Stamford, CT

PREP: 10 MIN. + FREEZING • **MAKES:** 10 POPS

- 1¾ cups whole milk, divided
- 1 to 2 Tbsp. honey
- ¼ tsp. vanilla extract
- 1½ cups fresh raspberries
- 1 cup fresh blueberries
- 10 freezer pop molds or 10 paper cups (3 oz. each) and wooden pop sticks

1. In a microwave, warm ¼ cup milk; stir in honey until blended. Stir in remaining 1½ cups milk and vanilla.

2. Divide berries among molds; cover with milk mixture. Top the molds with holders. If using cups, top with foil and insert sticks through the foil. Freeze until firm.

1 pop: 51 cal., 2g fat (1g sat. fat), 4mg chol., 19mg sod., 8g carb. (6g sugars, 2g fiber), 2g pro. **Diabetic exchanges:** ½ starch.

GRILLED PORK TENDERLOIN WITH CHERRY SALSA MOLE

GRILLED PORK TENDERLOIN WITH CHERRY SALSA MOLE

The combination of pork and cherries has long been a favorite of mine. The hint of spice and chocolate in the salsa mole makes the combination even more special.
—Roxanne Chan, Albany, CA

PREP: 25 MIN. • **GRILL:** 15 MIN. + STANDING
MAKES: 6 SERVINGS

  2   pork tenderloins (¾ lb. each)
  1   Tbsp. canola oil
  ½   tsp. salt
  ¼   tsp. ground cumin
  ¼   tsp. chili powder
  1   cup pitted fresh or frozen dark sweet cherries, thawed, chopped
  1   jalapeno pepper, seeded and minced
  ½   cup finely chopped peeled jicama
  1   oz. semisweet chocolate, grated
  2   Tbsp. minced fresh cilantro
  1   green onion, thinly sliced
  1   Tbsp. lime juice
  1   tsp. honey
    Salted pumpkin seeds or pepitas

1. Brush tenderloins with oil; sprinkle with salt, cumin and chili powder. Grill, meat covered, over medium heat until a thermometer reads 145°, 15-20 minutes, turning occasionally. Let meat stand 10-15 minutes.
2. Meanwhile, combine the cherries, jalapeno, jicama, chocolate, cilantro, green onion, lime juice and honey. Slice pork; serve with cherry salsa and pumpkin seeds.
3 oz. cooked pork with ¼ cup salsa:
218 cal., 8g fat (3g sat. fat), 64mg chol., 248mg sod., 11g carb. (9g sugars, 2g fiber), 23g pro. **Diabetic exchanges:** 3 lean meat, ½ starch, ½ fat.

SUMMER'S FAVORITE

VEGGIE DISHES

Juicy tomatoes enjoyed right off the vine, buttery cobs of corn seasoned to perfection, and brilliant peppers that spark up any dish—it's time to sink your teeth into the colorful veggies you've been anticipating all year long.

GRILLED
VEGETABLE
PLATTER

GRILLED VEGETABLE PLATTER

The best of summer in one dish! Grilling brings out veggies' natural sweetness, and the easy marinade really perks up the flavor.
—Heidi Hall, North St. Paul, MN

PREP: 20 MIN. + MARINATING • **GRILL:** 10 MIN.
MAKES: 6 SERVINGS

- ¼ cup olive oil
- 2 Tbsp. honey
- 4 tsp. balsamic vinegar
- 1 tsp. dried oregano
- ½ tsp. garlic powder
- ⅛ tsp. pepper
  Dash salt
- 1 lb. fresh asparagus, trimmed
- 3 small carrots, cut in half lengthwise
- 1 large sweet red pepper, cut into 1-in. strips
- 1 medium yellow summer squash, cut into ½-in. slices
- 1 medium red onion, cut into wedges

1. In a small bowl, whisk the first 7 ingredients. Place 3 Tbsp. marinade in a large resealable container. Add vegetables; seal container and turn to coat. Marinate vegetables 1½ hours at room temperature.
2. Transfer the vegetables to a grilling grid; place grid on grill rack. Grill the vegetables, covered, over medium heat 8-12 minutes or until crisp-tender, turning occasionally.
3. Place vegetables on a large serving plate. Drizzle with remaining marinade.
1 serving: 144 cal., 9g fat (1g sat. fat), 0 chol., 50mg sod., 15g carb. (11g sugars, 3g fiber), 2g pro. **Diabetic exchanges:** 2 vegetable, 2 fat.

If you don't have a grilling grid, try a disposable foil pan. Use a meat fork to poke holes in the bottom of the pan to allow liquid to drain.

EGGPLANT PARMESAN

EGGPLANT PARMESAN

We really like eggplant, but we would rather have it baked than fried. This can be served as a side or main dish.
—Donna Wardlow-Keating, Omaha, NE

PREP: 10 MIN. • **BAKE:** 45 MIN. + COOLING
MAKES: 2 SERVINGS

- 2 Tbsp. olive oil
- 1 garlic clove, minced
- 1 small eggplant, peeled and cut into ¼-in. slices
- 1 Tbsp. minced fresh basil or 1 tsp. dried basil
- 1 Tbsp. grated Parmesan cheese
- 1 medium tomato, thinly sliced
- ½ cup shredded mozzarella cheese
  Additional basil, optional

1. Combine oil and garlic; brush over both sides of eggplant slices. Place on a greased baking sheet. Bake at 425° for 15 minutes; turn. Bake until golden brown, about 5 minutes longer. Cool on a wire rack.
2. Place half of the eggplant in a greased 1-qt. baking dish. Sprinkle with half of the basil and Parmesan cheese. Arrange the tomato slices over top; sprinkle with remaining basil and Parmesan. Layer with half of the mozzarella cheese and remaining eggplant; top with remaining mozzarella. Cover and bake at 350° for 20 minutes. Uncover; bake until cheese is melted, 5-7 minutes longer. Garnish with additional basil if desired.
1 serving: 275 cal., 21g fat (6g sat. fat), 24mg chol., 164mg sod., 16g carb. (9g sugars, 5g fiber), 9g pro.

You do not need to peel young, tender eggplants before using. However, larger eggplants may be bitter and will taste better when peeled.

⑤

EASY GRILLED CORN WITH CHIPOTLE-LIME BUTTER

Grilling corn in the husks is so easy. There's no need to remove the silk and tie the husk closed before grilling. Just soak, grill and add your favorite flavored butter.
—*Taste of Home* Test Kitchen

PREP: 5 MIN. + SOAKING • **GRILL:** 25 MIN.
MAKES: 8 SERVINGS

- 8 large ears sweet corn in husks
- ½ cup butter, softened
- 1½ tsp. grated lime zest
- 1 tsp. minced fresh cilantro
- ½ tsp. salt
- ½ tsp. ground chipotle pepper
   Coarse sea salt, optional

1. In a large stockpot, cover corn with cold water. Soak for 30 minutes; drain. Grill corn, covered, over medium heat until tender, turning cobs occasionally, 25-30 minutes.
2. Meanwhile, combine the remaining ingredients.
3. Carefully peel back husks; discard silk. Spread the butter mixture over corn.
1 ear of corn with 2 Tbsp. butter: 225 cal., 13g fat (8g sat. fat), 31mg chol., 265mg sod., 27g carb. (9g sugars, 3g fiber), 5g pro.

⑤ ⑤

GRILLED CAULIFLOWER WEDGES

This meal is incredibly easy, yet is packed with flavor and looks like a dish from a five-star restaurant. The grill leaves the cauliflower cooked but crisp, and the red pepper flakes add bite.
—Carmel Hall, San Francisco, CA

TAKES: 30 MIN. • **MAKES:** 8 SERVINGS

- 1 large head cauliflower
- 1 tsp. ground turmeric
- ½ tsp. crushed red pepper flakes
- 2 Tbsp. olive oil
   Optional: Lemon juice, additional olive oil and pomegranate seeds

1. Remove leaves and trim stem from the cauliflower. Cut the cauliflower into 8 wedges. Mix the turmeric and pepper flakes. Brush wedges with oil; sprinkle with turmeric mixture.
2. Grill, covered, over medium-high heat or broil 4 in. from heat until cauliflower is tender, 8-10 minutes on each side. If desired, drizzle with lemon juice and additional oil and serve with pomegranate seeds.
1 wedge: 57 cal., 4g fat (1g sat. fat), 0 chol., 32mg sod., 5g carb. (2g sugars, 2g fiber), 2g pro. **Diabetic exchanges:** 1 vegetable, 1 fat.

⑤

GRILLED GREEN BEANS

I cook almost everything outdoors, including green beans. I prepare this snappy side dish while the entree is cooking. The recipe has won over my picky eaters.
—Carol Traupman-Carr, Breinigsville, PA

PREP: 25 MIN. • **GRILL:** 10 MIN.
MAKES: 4 SERVINGS

- 1 lb. fresh green beans, trimmed
- 2 Tbsp. butter
- 1 small shallot, minced
- 1 garlic clove, minced
- ½ cup grated Parmesan cheese

1. In a 6-qt. stockpot, bring 4 qt. water to a boil. Add beans; cook, uncovered, 2-3 minutes or until just crisp-tender. Remove beans and immediately drop into ice water.
2. In a small skillet, melt butter over medium-high heat. Add shallot; cook and stir 2-3 minutes or until lightly browned. Add garlic; cook 30 seconds longer. Remove from heat. Drain the beans and pat dry.
3. In a large bowl, combine the beans, shallot mixture and cheese; toss to coat. Transfer to a piece of heavy-duty foil (about 18-in. square) coated with cooking spray. Fold the foil around the beans, sealing tightly.
4. Grill, covered, over medium heat or broil 4 in. from heat 7-9 minutes or until cheese is melted. Open foil carefully to allow steam to escape.
1 cup: 137 cal., 9g fat (5g sat. fat), 24mg chol., 234mg sod., 12g carb. (3g sugars, 2g fiber), 5g pro.

GRILLED CABBAGE

I don't really like cabbage, but I tried this recipe and couldn't believe how good it was! We threw some burgers on the grill and our dinner was complete. I never thought I'd skip dessert because I was full from eating too much cabbage!

—Elizabeth Wheeler, Thornville, OH

TAKES: 30 MIN. • **MAKES:** 8 SERVINGS

- 1 medium head cabbage (about 1½ lbs.)
- ⅓ cup butter, softened
- ¼ cup chopped onion
- ½ tsp. garlic salt
- ¼ tsp. pepper

1. Cut cabbage into 8 wedges; place on a double thickness of heavy-duty foil (about 24 in. x 12 in.). Spread cut sides with butter. Sprinkle with onion, garlic salt and pepper.
2. Fold foil around the cabbage and seal tightly. Grill, covered, over medium heat for 20 minutes or until tender. Open foil carefully to allow steam to escape.
1 wedge: 98 cal., 8g fat (5g sat. fat), 20mg chol., 188mg sod., 7g carb. (4g sugars, 3g fiber), 2g pro. **Diabetic exchanges:** 1½ fat, 1 vegetable.

REFRIGERATOR GARDEN PICKLES

Canning isn't necessary for these crisp-tender, tangy pickles; they'll keep in the fridge for up to a month.

—Linda Chapman, Meriden, IA

PREP: 20 MIN. • **COOK:** 15 MIN. + CHILLING
MAKES: 7 PINTS

- 6 cups sugar
- 6 cups white vinegar
- ¼ cup celery seed
- ¼ cup mustard seed
- 2 Tbsp. canning salt
- 10 medium carrots, halved lengthwise and cut into 2-in. pieces
- 3 medium cucumbers, sliced
- 3 medium sweet red peppers, cut into 1-in. pieces
- 2 large onions, halved and sliced
- 1 bunch green onions, cut into 2-in. pieces

1. In a Dutch oven, combine the first 5 ingredients; bring to a boil, stirring to dissolve sugar. Meanwhile, place the remaining ingredients in a large bowl.
2. Pour hot liquid over vegetables; cool. Transfer to jars if desired; cover tightly. Refrigerate for 6-8 hours before serving. Store in refrigerator for up to 1 month.
¼ cup: 55 cal., 0 fat (0 sat. fat), 0 chol., 28mg sod., 13g carb. (11g sugars, 1g fiber), 1g pro.

CHERRY TOMATO MOZZARELLA SAUTE

This side is fast to fix and full of flavor. The mix of cherry tomatoes and mozzarella makes it a perfect pairing for any main dish.

—Summer Jones, Pleasant Grove, UT

TAKES: 25 MIN. • **MAKES:** 4 SERVINGS

- 2 tsp. olive oil
- ¼ cup chopped shallots
- 1 tsp. minced fresh thyme
- 1 garlic clove, minced
- 2½ cups cherry tomatoes, halved
- ¼ tsp. salt
- ¼ tsp. pepper
- 4 oz. fresh mozzarella cheese cut into ½-in. cubes

In a large skillet, heat oil over medium-high heat; saute shallots with thyme until tender. Add the garlic; cook and stir for 1 minute. Stir in the tomatoes, salt and pepper; heat through. Remove from the heat; stir in cheese.
⅔ cup: 127 cal., 9g fat (4g sat. fat), 22mg chol., 194mg sod., 6g carb. (4g sugars, 2g fiber), 6g pro.

It's easy to mince a fresh garlic clove when you start by crushing the clove with the blade of a chef's knife. Once you crush it, peel away the skin and then use the knife to mince (or chop) the garlic.

ZUCCHINI IN DILL CREAM SAUCE

My husband and I were dairy farmers until we retired in 1967, so I always use fresh, real dairy products in my recipes. This creamy sauce combines all of our favorite foods!
—Josephine Vanden Heuvel, Hart, MI

TAKES: 30 MIN. • **MAKES:** 8 SERVINGS

- 7 cups unpeeled zucchini, cut into ¼-in. slices
- ¼ cup finely chopped onion
- ½ cup water
- 1 tsp. salt
- 1 tsp. chicken bouillon granules or 1 chicken bouillon cube
- ½ tsp. dill weed
- 2 Tbsp. butter, melted
- 2 tsp. sugar
- 1 tsp. lemon juice
- 2 Tbsp. all-purpose flour
- ¼ cup sour cream

1. In saucepan, combine zucchini, onion, water, salt, bouillon and dill; bring to a boil. Add butter, sugar and lemon juice; mix. Remove from heat; do not drain.
2. Combine the flour and sour cream; stir half the mixture into hot zucchini. Return to heat; add remaining cream mixture and cook until thickened.
¾ each: 73 cal., 4g fat (0 sat. fat), 11mg chol., 419mg sod., 8g carb. (0 sugars, 0 fiber), 2g pro. **Diabetic exchanges:** 1 vegetable, 1 fat.

OVEN-ROASTED TOMATOES

I love tomatoes, as they're both healthy and versatile. You can use these roasted tomatoes in sandwiches or omelets, or to top broiled chicken.
—Julie Tilney, Downey, CA

PREP: 20 MIN. • **BAKE:** 3 HOURS + COOLING
MAKES: 4 CUPS

- 20 plum tomatoes (about 5 lbs.)
- ¼ cup olive oil
- 5 tsp. Italian seasoning
- 2½ tsp. salt

1. Cut tomatoes into ½-in. slices. Brush with oil; sprinkle with Italian seasoning and salt.
2. Place on racks coated with cooking spray in foil-lined 15x10x1-in. baking pans. Bake, uncovered, at 325° for 3-3½ hours or until the tomatoes are shriveled and deep brown around the edges. Cool for 10-15 minutes. Serve warm or at room temperature.
3. Store in an airtight container in the refrigerator for up to 1 week.
Freeze option: Place in freezer container; freeze for up to 3 months. Bring tomatoes to room temperature before using.
¼ cup: 45 cal., 4g fat (0 sat. fat), 0 chol., 373mg sod., 3g carb. (2g sugars, 1g fiber), 1g pro.

SPICY GRILLED EGGPLANT

This grilled side goes well with pasta—or meats also cooked on the grill. Thanks to the Cajun seasoning, the eggplant makes more of an impact than an ordinary veggie.
—Greg Fontenot, The Woodlands, TX

TAKES: 20 MIN. • **MAKES:** 8 SERVINGS

- 2 small eggplants, cut into ½-in. slices
- ¼ cup olive oil
- 2 Tbsp. lime juice
- 3 tsp. Cajun seasoning

1. Brush eggplant slices with oil. Drizzle with lime juice; sprinkle with the Cajun seasoning. Let stand 5 minutes.
2. Grill eggplant, covered, over medium heat or broil 4 in. from heat until tender, 4-5 minutes per side.
1 serving: 88 cal., 7g fat (1g sat. fat), 0 chol., 152mg sod., 7g carb. (3g sugars, 4g fiber), 1g pro. **Diabetic exchanges:** 1½ fat, 1 vegetable.

HEIRLOOM TOMATO PIE

HEIRLOOM TOMATO PIE

My green-thumb neighbors share produce with me. I return the favor by baking tomato pies for everybody.
—Angela Benedict, Dunbar, WV

PREP: 45 MIN. • **BAKE:** 35 MIN. + COOLING
MAKES: 8 SERVINGS

- 1¼ lbs. heirloom tomatoes (about 4 medium), cut into ¼-in. slices
- ¾ tsp. salt, divided
- 1½ cups shredded extra-sharp cheddar cheese
- ¾ cup all-purpose flour
- ¼ cup cold butter, cubed
- 1 to 2 Tbsp. half-and-half cream
- 5 bacon strips, cooked and crumbled

FILLING
- 1 pkg. (8 oz.) cream cheese, softened
- ½ cup loosely packed basil leaves, thinly sliced
- 2 Tbsp. minced fresh marjoram
- 1½ tsp. minced fresh thyme
- ½ tsp. garlic powder
- ⅛ tsp. coarsely ground pepper

1. Preheat oven to 350°. Place tomato slices in a single layer on paper towels; sprinkle with ½ tsp. salt. Let stand 45 minutes. Pat dry.

2. Meanwhile, place cheese, flour and remaining salt in a food processor; pulse until blended. Add the butter; pulse until butter is the size of peas. While pulsing, add just enough cream to form moist crumbs. Press dough onto bottom and up side of an ungreased 9-in. fluted tart pan with removable bottom. Gently press the bacon into the dough. Bake 20-22 minutes or until light brown. Cool on a wire rack.

3. In a large bowl, beat cream cheese, herbs and garlic powder until blended. Spread over crust. Top with tomato slices; sprinkle with pepper. Bake 35-40 minutes longer or until edges are golden brown and tomatoes are softened. Cool pie on a wire rack. Refrigerate leftovers.

1 piece: 320 cal., 25g fat (14g sat. fat), 74mg chol., 603mg sod., 14g carb. (3g sugars, 1g fiber), 11g pro.

Heirloom tomatoes sometimes have unconventional shapes. For best results, slice with a serrated knife.

YELLOW SQUASH & ZUCCHINI GRATIN

This gratin is the perfect way to use up an abundance of summer squash. It's easy to prepare, takes just 10 minutes in the oven, and serves up bubbly and delicious.
—Jonathan Lawler, Greenfield, IN

PREP: 25 MIN. • **BAKE:** 10 MIN.
MAKES: 6 SERVINGS

- 2 Tbsp. butter
- 2 medium zucchini, cut into ¼-in. slices
- 2 medium yellow summer squash, cut into ¼-in. slices
- 2 shallots, minced
- ½ tsp. sea salt
- ¼ tsp. coarsely ground pepper
- 4 garlic cloves, minced
- ½ cup heavy whipping cream
- 1 cup panko bread crumbs, divided
- ½ cup grated Parmesan cheese, divided

1. Preheat oven to 450°. In a large skillet, melt the butter over medium heat; add zucchini, yellow squash and shallots. Sprinkle with the salt and pepper. Cook, stirring occasionally, until zucchini and squash are crisp-tender, 4-6 minutes. Add garlic; cook 1 minute more.
2. Add the cream; cook until thickened, 3-5 minutes. Remove from heat; stir in ½ cup bread crumbs and ¼ cup cheese. Spoon mixture into a greased 11x7-in. or 2-qt. baking dish. Sprinkle with the remaining bread crumbs and cheese. Bake until golden brown, 8-10 minutes.
1 cup: 203 cal., 14g fat (8g sat. fat), 39mg chol., 357mg sod., 15g carb. (4g sugars, 2g fiber), 6g pro.

MEXICAN STREET CORN BAKE

🄵 MEXICAN STREET CORN BAKE

We discovered Mexican street corn at a festival. This easy one-pan version saves on prep and cleanup. Every August, I freeze a lot of our own fresh sweet corn, and I use that in this recipe, but store-bought corn works just as well.
—Erin Wright, Wallace, KS

PREP: 10 MIN. • **BAKE:** 35 MIN.
MAKES: 6 SERVINGS

- 6 cups frozen corn (about 30 oz.), thawed and drained
- 1 cup mayonnaise
- 1 tsp. ground chipotle pepper
- ¼ tsp. salt
- ¼ tsp. pepper
- 6 Tbsp. chopped green onions, divided
- ½ cup grated Parmesan cheese
  Lime wedges, optional

1. Preheat oven to 350°. Mix the first 5 ingredients and 4 Tbsp. green onions; transfer to a greased 1½-qt. baking dish. Sprinkle with cheese.
2. Bake, covered, 20 minutes. Uncover; bake until bubbly and lightly browned, 15-20 minutes. Sprinkle with remaining green onions. If desired, serve with lime wedges.
⅔ cup: 391 cal., 30g fat (5g sat. fat), 8mg chol., 423mg sod., 30g carb. (4g sugars, 3g fiber), 6g pro.

GRILLED MUSHROOM KABOBS

ASPARAGUS, SQUASH & RED PEPPER SAUTE

The flavor of this appealing vegetable trio is enhanced by a delicate wine saute.
—Deirdre Cox, Kansas City, MO

TAKES: 30 MIN. • **MAKES:** 4 SERVINGS

- 2 medium sweet red peppers, julienned
- 2 medium yellow summer squash, halved lengthwise and cut into ¼-in. slices
- 6 oz. fresh asparagus, trimmed and cut into 1½-in. pieces
- ¼ cup white wine or ¼ cup vegetable broth
- 4½ tsp. olive oil
- ¼ tsp. salt
- ¼ tsp. pepper

In a large cast-iron or other heavy skillet, saute peppers, squash and asparagus in wine and oil until crisp-tender. Sprinkle with salt and pepper.

¾ cup: 90 cal., 5g fat (1g sat. fat), 0 chol., 163mg sod., 8g carb. (5g sugars, 3g fiber), 2g pro. **Diabetic exchanges:** 1 vegetable, 1 fat.

This recipe is adaptable, so feel free to use your favorite summer produce. Try it with zucchini, corn or even fresh green beans.

GRILLED MUSHROOM KABOBS

Earthy grilled mushrooms taste like flame-kissed goodness. The balsamic vinegar adds just the right tangy flavor to this savory side.
—Melissa Hoddinott, Sherwood Park, AB

PREP: 30 MIN. • **COOK:** 10 MIN.
MAKES: 4 SERVINGS

- 16 pearl onions
- 20 medium fresh mushrooms
- ⅓ cup balsamic vinegar
- ¼ cup butter, cubed
- 2 garlic cloves, minced
- ½ tsp. salt
- ½ tsp. pepper
  Minced fresh parsley, optional

1. In a small saucepan, bring 6 cups water to a boil. Add pearl onions; boil 5 minutes. Drain and rinse with cold water. Peel.

2. Using 4 metal or soaked wooden skewers, alternately thread mushrooms and onions, piercing the mushrooms horizontally through the caps. In a microwave-safe bowl, combine the vinegar, butter, garlic, salt and pepper; microwave mixture, covered, on high for 30-45 seconds or until butter is melted. Whisk to combine. Reserve half of the vinegar mixture for serving. Brush the kabobs with remaining vinegar mixture.

3. Grill the kabobs, covered, over medium heat or broil 4 in. from heat 10-12 minutes or until vegetables are tender, turning occasionally and basting frequently with the vinegar mixture. If desired, sprinkle with parsley. Serve with reserved vinegar mixture.

1 kabob: 161 cal., 12g fat (7g sat. fat), 31mg chol., 393mg sod., 13g carb. (7g sugars, 1g fiber), 3g pro.

SUMMER'S EASIEST

WEEKNIGHT ENTREES

It's easy to keep the spotlight on seasonal favorites with these no-fuss dinners. You'll keep the kitchen cool and step into summer fun fast with 30-minute dinners, main-dish salads, grilled greats and other workweek staples.

TZATZIKI
CHICKEN

TZATZIKI CHICKEN

I like to make classic chicken recipes for my family but the real fun is trying a fresh new twist like this.
—Kristen Heigl, Staten Island, NY

TAKES: 30 MIN. • **MAKES:** 4 SERVINGS

- 1½ cups finely chopped peeled English cucumber
- 1 cup plain Greek yogurt
- 2 garlic cloves, minced
- 1½ tsp. chopped fresh dill
- 1½ tsp. olive oil
- ⅛ tsp. salt

CHICKEN
- ⅔ cup all-purpose flour
- 1 tsp. salt
- 1 tsp. pepper
- ¼ tsp. baking powder
- 1 large egg
- ⅓ cup 2% milk
- 4 boneless skinless chicken breast halves (6 oz. each)
- ¼ cup canola oil
- ¼ cup crumbled feta cheese
  Lemon wedges, optional

1. For sauce, mix the first 6 ingredients; refrigerate until serving.
2. In a shallow bowl, whisk together the flour, salt, pepper and baking powder. In another bowl, whisk together egg and milk. Pound chicken breasts with a meat mallet to ½-in. thickness. Dip in flour mixture to coat both sides; shake off excess. Dip in egg mixture, then again in flour mixture.
3. In a large skillet, heat oil over medium heat. Cook chicken 5-7 minutes per side or until golden brown and chicken is no longer pink. Top with cheese. Serve with the sauce and, if desired, lemon wedges.
1 chicken breast half with ⅓ cup sauce: 482 cal., 27g fat (7g sat. fat), 133mg chol., 737mg sod., 17g carb. (4g sugars, 1g fiber), 41g pro.

An English cucumber works well in this recipe because it's seedless and doesn't thin out the sauce. A regular cucumber can be used, too; just seed it before chopping.

CALIFORNIA BURGER BOWLS

CALIFORNIA BURGER BOWLS

Burgers are a weekly staple at our house all year round. Skip the fries, chips and bun—you won't need them with these loaded veggie and fruit burgers. To spice up the mayo, add half a teaspoon chipotle powder.
—Courtney Stultz, Weir, KS

TAKES: 25 MIN. • **MAKES:** 4 SERVINGS

- 3 Tbsp. fat-free milk
- 2 Tbsp. quick-cooking oats
- ¾ tsp. salt
- ½ tsp. ground cumin
- ½ tsp. chili powder
- ½ tsp. pepper
- 1 lb. lean ground turkey
- 4 cups baby kale salad blend
- 1½ cups cubed fresh pineapple (½ in.)
- 1 medium mango, peeled and thinly sliced
- 1 medium ripe avocado, peeled and thinly sliced
- 1 medium sweet red pepper, cut into strips
- 4 tomatillos, husks removed, thinly sliced
- ¼ cup reduced-fat chipotle mayonnaise

1. In a large bowl, mix milk, oats and seasonings. Add the turkey; mix lightly but thoroughly. Shape into four ½-in.-thick patties.
2. Place burgers on an oiled grill rack over medium heat. Grill, covered, until a thermometer reads 165°, 4-5 minutes per side. Serve over salad blend, along with remaining ingredients.
1 serving: 390 cal., 19g fat (4g sat. fat), 83mg chol., 666mg sod., 33g carb. (22g sugars, 7g fiber), 26g pro. **Diabetic exchanges:** 3 lean meat, 2½ fat, 2 vegetable, 1 fruit.

Save even more time when you top the burger bowls with prepared guacamole instead of the spicy chipotle mayonnaise.

CRAB-TOPPED FISH FILLETS

Elegant but truly no bother, this recipe is perfect for company. Toasting the almonds gives them a little more crunch, which is a delightful way to top the fish fillets.
—Mary Tuthill, Fort Myers Beach, FL

TAKES: 30 MIN. • **MAKES:** 4 SERVINGS

- 4 sole or cod fillets or fish fillets of your choice (6 oz. each)
- 1 can (6 oz.) crabmeat, drained and flaked, or 1 cup imitation crabmeat, chopped
- ½ cup grated Parmesan cheese
- ½ cup mayonnaise
- 1 tsp. lemon juice
- ⅓ cup slivered almonds, toasted Paprika, optional

1. Place the fillets in a greased 13x9-in. baking dish. Bake, uncovered, at 350° for 18-22 minutes or until fish flakes easily with a fork. Meanwhile, in a large bowl, combine the crab, cheese, mayonnaise and lemon juice.
2. Drain cooking juices from baking dish; spoon crab mixture over fillets. Broil 4-5 in. from heat for 5 minutes or until topping is lightly browned. Sprinkle with almonds and paprika if desired.
1 fillet: 429 cal., 31g fat (6g sat. fat), 128mg chol., 1063mg sod., 3g carb. (0 sugars, 1g fiber), 33g pro.

SOUTHWEST
TORTILLA-TURKEY SKILLET

SOUTHWEST TORTILLA-TURKEY SKILLET

I wanted to cut back on red meat, but my husband thinks ground turkey can be dry. I think the taco seasoning and jalapeno juice in this recipe give the turkey added flavor and moistness, and he agrees.
—Lindsay Ludden, Omaha, NE

TAKES: 25 MIN. • **MAKES:** 2 SERVINGS

- ½ lb. ground turkey
- ¾ cup black beans, rinsed and drained
- ½ cup water
- ⅓ cup sliced ripe olives
- 2 Tbsp. reduced-sodium taco seasoning
- 1 Tbsp. juice from pickled jalapeno slices
- 1 flour tortilla (10 in.), cut into 1-in. pieces
- ½ cup shredded reduced-fat Mexican cheese blend
- 2 Tbsp. pickled jalapeno slices
- 2 Tbsp. reduced-fat sour cream

1. In a large skillet, cook turkey over medium heat until no longer pink; drain. Stir in the beans, water, olives, taco seasoning and juice from jalapenos. Bring to a boil. Reduce heat; simmer, uncovered, for 6-7 minutes or until mixture is thickened.
2. Stir in tortilla pieces. Sprinkle with cheese and jalapeno. Remove from heat and cover for 1-2 minutes or until cheese is melted. Serve with sour cream.
1½ cups: 496 cal., 21g fat (8g sat. fat), 91mg chol., 1502mg sod., 41g carb. (6g sugars, 6g fiber), 39g pro.

TEQUILA LIME SHRIMP ZOODLES

This tangy shrimp is a great way to cut carbs without sacrificing flavor. If you don't have a spiralizer, use thinly julienned zucchini to get a similar effect.

—Brigette Schroeder, Yorkville, IL

TAKES: 30 MIN. • **MAKES:** 4 SERVINGS

- 3 Tbsp. butter, divided
- 1 shallot, minced
- 2 garlic cloves, minced
- ¼ cup tequila
- 1½ tsp. grated lime zest
- 2 Tbsp. lime juice
- 1 Tbsp. olive oil
- 1 lb. uncooked shrimp (31-40 per lb.), peeled and deveined
- 2 medium zucchini, spiralized (about 6 cups)
- ½ tsp. salt
- ¼ tsp. pepper
- ¼ cup minced fresh parsley
  Additional grated lime zest

1. In a large skillet, heat 2 Tbsp. butter over medium heat. Add the shallot and garlic; cook 1-2 minutes. Remove from heat; stir in tequila, lime zest and lime juice. Cook over medium heat until liquid is almost evaporated, 2-3 minutes.
2. Add olive oil and remaining butter; stir in shrimp and zucchini. Sprinkle with salt and pepper. Cook and stir until shrimp begin to turn pink and the zucchini is crisp-tender, 4-5 minutes. Sprinkle with parsley and additional lime zest.

1¼ cups: 246 cal., 14g fat (6g sat. fat), 161mg chol., 510mg sod., 7g carb. (3g sugars, 1g fiber), 20g pro. **Diabetic exchanges:** 3 lean meat, 3 fat, 1 vegetable.

EASY STUFFED POBLANOS

My partner adores these saucy stuffed peppers—and I love how quickly they come together. Top with low-fat sour cream and your favorite salsa.

—Jean Erhardt, Portland, OR

TAKES: 25 MIN. • **MAKES:** 4 SERVINGS

- ½ lb. Italian turkey sausage links, casings removed
- ½ lb. lean ground beef (90% lean)
- 1 pkg. (8.8 oz.) ready-to-serve Spanish rice
- 4 large poblano peppers
- 1 cup enchilada sauce
- ½ cup shredded Mexican cheese blend
  Minced fresh cilantro, optional

1. Preheat broiler.
2. In a large skillet, cook the turkey and beef over medium heat until no longer pink, 5-7 minutes, breaking meat into crumbles; drain.
3. Prepare rice according to package directions. Add rice to meat mixture.
4. Cut the peppers lengthwise in half; remove seeds. Place on a foil-lined 15x10x1-in. baking pan, cut side down. Broil 4 in. from heat until the skins blister, about 5 minutes. With tongs, turn the peppers.
5. Fill with the turkey mixture; top with enchilada sauce and sprinkle with cheese. Broil 1-2 minutes longer or until cheese is melted. If desired, top with cilantro.

2 stuffed pepper halves: 312 cal., 13g fat (4g sat. fat), 63mg chol., 1039mg sod., 27g carb. (5g sugars, 2g fiber), 22g pro.

Prepared Spanish rice adds so much flavor with so little effort! If you have leftover Spanish rice, use about 2 cups cooked rice for the filling.

**PAN-SEARED SALMON
WITH DILL SAUCE**

2. Remove from heat; let stand
5 minutes. If desired, top with parsley.
Note: This recipe was tested with
McCormick Gourmet Moroccan
Seasoning (ras el hanout).
1 cup: 335 cal., 11g fat (1g sat. fat), 138mg
chol., 626mg sod., 34g carb. (1g sugars,
1g fiber), 24g pro.

THAI PEANUT NAAN PIZZAS

*I'm a huge fan of Thai food, but don't always
have the time to make it at home. To get my
fix, I top fluffy naan bread with a ginger-
peanut sauce, fresh veggies, a sprinkle of
cilantro and a spicy squiggle of Sriracha.*
—Rachel Bernhard Seis, Milwaukee, WI

TAKES: 25 MIN. • **MAKES:** 4 SERVINGS

- ¼ cup creamy peanut butter
- 3 Tbsp. sesame ginger salad
  dressing
- 1 Tbsp. water
- 1 tsp. soy sauce
- 2 naan flatbreads
- 1 cup shredded part-skim
  mozzarella cheese
- 1 small sweet red pepper, julienned
- ½ cup julienned carrot
- ½ cup sliced baby portobello
  mushrooms
- ¼ cup chopped fresh cilantro
  Sriracha chili sauce, optional

1. Preheat oven to 425°. For sauce, mix
first 4 ingredients until blended. Place
naan on a baking sheet; spread with
sauce. Top with cheese and vegetables.
2. Bake until cheese is melted and crust
is golden brown, 8-10 minutes. Top with
the cilantro and, if desired, drizzle with
chili sauce.
½ pizza: 316 cal., 19g fat (6g sat. fat), 21mg
chol., 698mg sod., 25g carb. (8g sugars, 2g
fiber), 13g pro.

To wash cilantro, dunk or
soak in a deep container
of water to allow any dirt
or grit to settle on the
bottom, changing out the
water 2-3 times. Gently
blot the leaves dry
and proceed with the
recipe as directed.

PAN-SEARED SALMON
WITH DILL SAUCE

*This is one of my husband's favorite recipes.
Salmon is a go-to for busy nights because
it cooks so quickly and goes with so many
different flavors. The creamy dill sauce
tastes light and fresh, with a nice crunch
from the cucumbers.*
—Angela Spengler, Niceville, FL

TAKES: 25 MIN. • **MAKES:** 4 SERVINGS

- 1 Tbsp. canola oil
- 4 salmon fillets (6 oz. each)
- 1 tsp. Italian seasoning
- ¼ tsp. salt
- ½ cup reduced-fat plain yogurt
- ¼ cup reduced-fat mayonnaise
- ¼ cup finely chopped cucumber
- 1 tsp. snipped fresh dill

1. In a large skillet, heat oil over medium-
high heat. Sprinkle salmon with Italian
seasoning and salt. Place in skillet, skin
side down. Reduce heat to medium. Cook
until fish just begins to flake easily with a
fork, about 5 minutes on each side.
2. Meanwhile, in a small bowl, combine
yogurt, mayonnaise, cucumber and dill.
Serve with salmon.
1 salmon fillet with ¼ cup sauce: 366 cal.,
25g fat (4g sat. fat), 92mg chol., 349mg
sod., 4g carb. (3g sugars, 0 fiber), 31g pro.
Diabetic exchanges: 4 lean meat, 2½ fat.

QUICK MOROCCAN
SHRIMP SKILLET

*When my niece was attending West Point,
she was sent to Morocco for five months. I
threw her a going-away party with Moroccan
decorations, costumes and cuisine, including
this saucy shrimp dish. Whenever I make it
now, I think of her and I smile.*
—Barbara Lento, Houston, PA

TAKES: 25 MIN. • **MAKES:** 4 SERVINGS

- 1 Tbsp. canola oil
- 1 small onion, chopped
- ¼ cup pine nuts
- 1 lb. uncooked shrimp (16-20 per lb.),
  peeled and deveined
- 1 cup uncooked pearl (Israeli)
  couscous
- 2 Tbsp. lemon juice
- 3 tsp. Moroccan seasoning
  (ras el hanout)
- 1 tsp. garlic salt
- 2 cups hot water
  Minced fresh parsley, optional

1. In a large skillet, heat oil over medium-
high heat; saute onion and pine nuts until
onion is tender, 2-3 minutes. Stir in all
remaining ingredients except parsley;
bring just to a boil. Reduce heat; simmer,
covered, 4-6 minutes or until the shrimp
turn pink.

THAI PEANUT
NAAN PIZZAS

SOUTHWESTERN FISH TACOS

These bright tacos take me on an instant trip to sunny Southern California. This recipe has been on my family's most-requested list for many years.

—Joan Hallford, North Richland Hills, TX

TAKES: 20 MIN.
MAKES: 2 SERVINGS (4 TACOS)

¼ cup mayonnaise
¼ cup sour cream
2 Tbsp. minced fresh cilantro
4 tsp. taco seasoning
½ lb. cod or haddock fillets, cut into 1-in. pieces
1 Tbsp. lemon juice
1 Tbsp. canola oil
4 taco shells
Optional ingredients: shredded lettuce, chopped tomato and lime wedges

1. For the sauce, mix the mayonnaise, sour cream, cilantro and 2 tsp. taco seasoning. In another bowl, toss the cod with lemon juice and remaining taco seasoning.
2. In a skillet, heat oil over medium-high heat; saute the cod just until it begins to flake easily with a fork, 4-6 minutes (fish may break apart as it cooks). Spoon into the taco shells; serve with sauce and remaining ingredients as desired.
2 tacos: 506 cal., 38g fat (8g sat. fat), 52mg chol., 852mg sod., 20g carb. (1g sugars, 1g fiber), 20g pro.

CARAMELIZED PORK SLICES

This easy treatment for pork caught my eye when I was thumbing through a cookbook and saw the word "caramelized." I like to serve this over noodles or rice, or alongside mashed potatoes.

—Elisa Lochridge, Beaverton, OR

TAKES: 25 MIN. • **MAKES:** 4 SERVINGS

1 pork tenderloin (1 lb.)
2 tsp. canola oil, divided
2 garlic cloves, minced
2 Tbsp. brown sugar
1 Tbsp. orange juice
1 Tbsp. molasses
½ tsp. salt
¼ tsp. pepper

1. Cut tenderloin into 8 slices; pound each with a meat mallet to a ½-in. thickness. In a nonstick skillet, heat 1 tsp. oil over medium-high heat; brown pork on both sides. Remove from pan.
2. In same skillet, heat the remaining oil over medium-high heat; saute garlic 1 minute. Stir in remaining ingredients. Add the pork, turning to coat; cook, uncovered, until a thermometer inserted in pork reads 145°, 3-4 minutes. Let stand 5 minutes before serving.
2 pork slices: 198 cal., 6g fat (2g sat. fat), 64mg chol., 344mg sod., 12g carb. (11g sugars, 0 fiber), 23g pro. **Diabetic exchanges:** 3 lean meat, ½ starch.

SAUSAGE COBB SALAD LETTUCE WRAPS

I substituted sausage for the bacon to make this lettuce roll-up your family and friends will adore. It's flavorful, crunchy and pretty on the plate.

—Devon Delaney, Westport, CT

TAKES: 25 MIN. • **MAKES:** 6 SERVINGS

¾ cup ranch salad dressing
⅓ cup crumbled blue cheese
¼ cup watercress, chopped
1 lb. bulk pork sausage
2 Tbsp. minced fresh chives
6 large iceberg lettuce leaves, edges trimmed
1 medium ripe avocado, peeled and diced
4 hard-boiled large eggs, chopped
1 medium tomato, chopped

1. Mix the dressing, blue cheese and watercress. In a large skillet, cook and crumble sausage over medium heat until no longer pink, 5-7 minutes; drain. Stir in the chives.
2. To serve, spoon sausage into lettuce leaves. Top with avocado, eggs and tomato. Drizzle with dressing mixture.
1 wrap: 433 cal., 38g fat (10g sat. fat), 174mg chol., 887mg sod., 7g carb. (3g sugars, 3g fiber), 15g pro.

SALSA BLACK BEAN BURGERS

Meatless meals are always extra tasty when these hearty bean burgers are on the menu. Guacamole and sour cream make it seem a bit decadent.
—Jill Reichardt, Saint Louis, MO

TAKES: 30 MIN. • **MAKES:** 4 SERVINGS

- 1   can (15 oz.) black beans, rinsed and drained
- ⅔ cup dry bread crumbs
- 1   small tomato, seeded and finely chopped
- 1   jalapeno pepper, seeded and finely chopped
- 1   large egg
- 1   tsp. minced fresh cilantro
- 1   garlic clove, minced
- 1   Tbsp. olive oil
- 4   whole wheat hamburger buns, split
     Optional: Reduced-fat sour cream and guacamole

1. Place beans in a food processor; cover and process until blended. Transfer to a large bowl. Add bread crumbs, tomato, jalapeno, egg, cilantro and garlic. Mix until combined. Shape into 4 patties.
2. In a large nonstick skillet, cook patties in oil in batches over medium heat until lightly browned, 4-6 minutes on each side. Serve on buns. If desired, top with sour cream and guacamole.
Note: Wear disposable gloves when cutting hot peppers; the oils can burn skin. Avoid touching your face.
1 burger: 323 cal., 8g fat (1g sat. fat), 53mg chol., 557mg sod., 51g carb. (6g sugars, 9g fiber), 13g pro.

BLT CHICKEN SALAD

Featuring all the fun fixings for a BLT chicken sandwich, this salad is so lovable. I can prep the ingredients ahead of time and just throw it together at the last minute. Barbecue sauce in the dressing gives it unexpected flavor. Even picky eaters love it.
—Cindy Moore, Mooresville, NC

TAKES: 20 MIN. • **MAKES:** 8 SERVINGS

- ½   cup mayonnaise
- 3   to 4 Tbsp. barbecue sauce
- 2   Tbsp. finely chopped onion
- 1   Tbsp. lemon juice
- ¼   tsp. pepper
- 8   cups torn salad greens
- 2   large tomatoes, chopped
- 1½ lbs. boneless skinless chicken breasts, cooked and cubed
- 10 bacon strips, cooked and crumbled
- 2   hard-boiled large eggs, sliced

In a small bowl, combine the first 5 ingredients; mix well. Cover and refrigerate until serving. Place salad greens in a large bowl. Sprinkle with tomatoes, chicken and bacon; garnish with eggs. Drizzle with dressing.
1 serving: 281 cal., 19g fat (4g sat. fat), 112mg chol., 324mg sod., 5g carb. (3g sugars, 2g fiber), 23g pro.

MARINATED STEAK WITH GRILLED ONIONS

This marinade is magic —it will make even economic cuts of beef tender and delicious.
—Gail Garcelon, Beaverton, OR

PREP: 10 MIN. + MARINATING
GRILL: 10 MIN.
MAKES: 12 SERVINGS (1 CUP COOKED ONIONS)

- 1¼ cups balsamic vinaigrette
- 4   tsp. ground mustard
- 2¼ tsp. Worcestershire sauce
- 2   garlic cloves, minced
- 3   beef top sirloin steaks (¾ in. thick and 1 lb. each)
- 5   medium onions, sliced

1. Whisk together vinaigrette, mustard, Worcestershire sauce and garlic. Pour ¼ cup into a shallow dish. Add the beef and turn to coat. Cover and refrigerate 6 hours or overnight. Cover and refrigerate remaining marinade.
2. Drain beef, discarding marinade in dish. Grill steaks and onions, covered, over medium heat or broil 4 in. from heat until meat reaches desired doneness (for medium-rare, a thermometer should read 135°; medium, 140°; medium-well, 145°) and onions are tender, 4-7 minutes per side. Drizzle reserved marinade over onions. Cut steak into thin slices; serve with onions.
3 oz. cooked beef with ⅛ cup onion slices: 209 cal., 8g fat (2g sat. fat), 46mg chol., 294mg sod., 6g carb. (3g sugars, 1g fiber), 25g pro. **Diabetic exchanges:** 3 lean meat.

SUMMER'S BEST

INSTANT POT®
& AIR-FRYER
RECIPES

Take advantage of your Instant Pot and air fryer to serve classic summer dishes with ease. These popular devices help you set satisfying meals on the kitchen table no matter how busy your schedule might be.

AIR-FRYER SHRIMP PO'BOYS

My husband loves crispy coconut shrimp and po'boys. I combined them, added a spicy remoulade—and voila! This air-fryer shrimp is a big hit with family and friends and is frequently requested. For a catfish po'boy, substitute cornmeal for the coconut and add a few minutes to the cooking time.
—Marla Clark, Albuquerque, NM

PREP: 35 MIN. • **COOK:** 10 MIN./BATCH
MAKES: 4 SERVINGS

- **½ cup mayonnaise**
- **1 Tbsp. Creole mustard**
- **1 Tbsp. chopped cornichons or dill pickles**
- **1 Tbsp. minced shallot**
- **1½ tsp. lemon juice**
- **⅛ tsp. cayenne pepper**

COCONUT SHRIMP

- **1 cup all-purpose flour**
- **1 tsp. herbes de Provence**
- **½ tsp. sea salt**
- **½ tsp. garlic powder**
- **½ tsp. pepper**
- **¼ tsp. cayenne pepper**
- **1 large egg**
- **½ cup 2% milk**
- **1 tsp. hot pepper sauce**
- **2 cups sweetened shredded coconut**
- **1 lb. uncooked shrimp (26-30 per lb.), peeled and deveined**
- **Cooking spray**
- **4 hoagie buns, split**
- **2 cups shredded lettuce**
- **1 medium tomato, thinly sliced**

1. For remoulade, in a small bowl, combine the first 6 ingredients. Refrigerate, covered, until serving.
2. Preheat air fryer to 375°. In a shallow bowl, mix flour, herbes de Provence, sea salt, garlic powder, pepper and cayenne. In a separate shallow bowl, whisk egg, milk and hot pepper sauce. Place the coconut in a third shallow bowl. Dip the shrimp in flour to coat both sides; shake off excess. Dip in the egg mixture, then in coconut, patting to help adhere.
3. In batches, arrange shrimp in a single layer in greased air-fryer basket; spritz with cooking spray. Cook until coconut is lightly browned and shrimp turn pink, 3-4 minutes on each side.
4. Spread the cut side of buns with the remoulade. Top the bottom bun with the shrimp, lettuce and tomato.

1 sandwich: 716 cal., 40g fat (16g sat. fat), 173mg chol., 944mg sod., 60g carb. (23g sugars, 4g fiber), 31g pro.

5i

PRESSURE-COOKED BBQ CHICKEN

When we can't barbecue on the grill, I bring out my pressure cooker for this fall-off-the-bone chicken. My jazzed-up barbecue sauce adds great flavor.
—Diane Hixon, Niceville, FL

PREP: 20 MIN. • **COOK:** 10 MIN. + COOLING
MAKES: 4 SERVINGS

- **2 Tbsp. canola oil**
- **1 broiler/fryer chicken (3 to 4 lbs.), cut up**
- **2 cups barbecue sauce**
- **1½ cups coarsely chopped onions**
- **1 large green pepper, chopped**
- **½ cup water**

1. Select saute or browning setting on a 6-qt. electric pressure cooker. Adjust for medium heat; add oil. When the oil is hot, brown chicken in batches. Press cancel. Return all to pressure cooker. Combine remaining ingredients. Pour mixture over the chicken.
2. Lock lid; close pressure-release valve. Adjust to pressure-cook on high for 10 minutes. Let the pressure release naturally. A thermometer inserted in a breast or thigh piece should read at least 170°. If desired, thicken cooking juices.

1 serving: 423 cal., 18g fat (4g sat. fat), 110mg chol., 1114mg sod., 24g carb. (19g sugars, 3g fiber), 40g pro.

PRESSURE-COOKER BEEF BURRITOS WITH GREEN CHILES

Here's a family favorite that makes mouths water with just its heavenly aroma! Hearty and flavorful, it's quick comfort food.
—Sally J. Pahler, Palisade, CO

PREP: 20 MIN.
COOK: 1 HOUR 20 MIN. + RELEASING
MAKES: 14 SERVINGS

> 4 cans (7 oz. each) whole green chiles, undrained
> 1 can (28 oz.) diced tomatoes, undrained
> 1 large onion, diced
> 1 boneless beef chuck roast (4 lbs.)
> 2 garlic cloves, minced
> 1 tsp. salt
> 2 tsp. ground cumin
> 1 tsp. cayenne pepper
> 14 whole wheat tortillas (8 in.), warmed
> Optional toppings: Shredded cheddar cheese, salsa, sour cream and sliced ripe olives

1. Drain chiles, reserving liquid. Coarsely chop the chiles; place in a 6-qt. electric pressure cooker. Add tomatoes, onion and reserved drained liquid. Cut roast in half. Combine the garlic, salt, cumin and cayenne; rub over roast. Place meat in the pressure cooker. Lock lid; close the pressure-release valve. Adjust to pressure-cook on high for 80 minutes. Let the pressure release naturally for 10 minutes; quick-release any remaining pressure. A thermometer inserted in beef should read at least 165°.
2. Remove roast; shred the roast with 2 forks. Return to pressure cooker; heat through. Using a slotted spoon, serve in tortillas. Add toppings as desired.
Freeze option: Freeze the cooled meat mixture and juices in freezer containers. To use, partially thaw in the refrigerator overnight. Heat through in a saucepan, stirring occasionally; add water if necessary.
1 burrito: 355 cal., 13g fat (5g sat. fat), 84mg chol., 499mg sod., 28g carb. (4g sugars, 4g fiber), 30g pro. **Diabetic exchanges:** 4 lean meat, 1 starch.

PRESSURE-COOKER BEEF BURRITOS WITH GREEN CHILES

5i
PRESSURE-COOKED MESQUITE RIBS

When we're missing the grill during winter, these tangy ribs give us that same smoky barbecue taste we love. They're so simple, tender and delicious!

—Sue Evans, Marquette, MI

PREP: 10 MIN. + BROILING
COOK: 35 MIN. + RELEASING
MAKES: 8 SERVINGS

- 1   cup water
- 2   Tbsp. cider vinegar
- 1   Tbsp. soy sauce
- 4   lbs. pork baby back ribs, cut into serving-size portions
- 2   Tbsp. mesquite seasoning
- ¾   cup barbecue sauce, divided

1. Combine water, vinegar and soy sauce in a 6-qt. electric pressure cooker. Rub the ribs with the mesquite seasoning; add to pressure cooker. Lock lid; close the pressure-release valve. Adjust to pressure-cook on high for 35 minutes. Allow pressure to naturally release for 10 minutes, then quick-release any remaining pressure.
2. Remove the ribs to a foil-lined baking sheet. Preheat broiler. Brush ribs with half of barbecue sauce. Broil 4-6 in. from heat until glazed. Brush with remaining barbecue sauce.

1 serving: 329 cal., 21g fat (8g sat. fat), 81mg chol., 678mg sod., 10g carb. (8g sugars, 0 fiber), 23g pro.

PRESSURE-COOKER CAROLINA-STYLE VINEGAR BBQ CHICKEN

5i
PRESSURE-COOKER CAROLINA-STYLE VINEGAR BBQ CHICKEN

I live in Georgia but I appreciate the tangy, sweet and slightly spicy taste of Carolina vinegar chicken.

—Ramona Parris, Canton, GA

TAKES: 25 MIN. • **MAKES:** 6 SERVINGS

- 2   cups water
- 1   cup white vinegar
- ¼   cup sugar
- 1   Tbsp. reduced-sodium chicken base
- 1   tsp. crushed red pepper flakes
- ¾   tsp. salt
- 1½   lbs. boneless skinless chicken breasts
- 6   whole wheat hamburger buns, split, optional

1. In a 6-qt. electric pressure cooker, mix the first 6 ingredients; add chicken. Lock the lid; close the pressure-release valve. Adjust to pressure-cook on high for 5 minutes.
2. Allow pressure to naturally release for 8 minutes, then quick-release any remaining pressure.
3. Remove chicken; cool slightly. Reserve 1 cup cooking juices; discard remaining juices. Shred the chicken with 2 forks. Combine with reserved juices. If desired, serve chicken mixture on buns.

½ cup: 135 cal., 3g fat (1g sat. fat), 63mg chol., 228mg sod., 3g carb. (3g sugars, 0 fiber), 23g pro. **Diabetic exchanges:** 3 lean meat.

PRESSURE-COOKER
CINNAMON BLUEBERRY
FRENCH TOAST

PRESSURE-COOKER CINNAMON BLUEBERRY FRENCH TOAST

Healthy and hearty! That's the best way to describe this satisfying breakfast. It's one dish worth jumping out of bed for.
—Angela Lively, Conroe, TX

PREP: 15 MIN. + STANDING
COOK: 20 MIN. + RELEASING
MAKES: 4 SERVINGS

- 2 large eggs
- 1⅓ cups 2% milk
- 3 Tbsp. sugar
- 1 tsp. ground cinnamon
- 1 tsp. vanilla extract
- ¼ tsp. salt
- 6 cups cubed French bread (about 6 oz.)
- ¾ cup fresh or frozen blueberries
  Maple syrup

1. Whisk together first 6 ingredients. Arrange half of the bread cubes in a greased 1½-qt. baking dish. Top with half the blueberries and half the milk mixture. Repeat layers.
2. Place trivet insert and 1 cup water in a 6-qt. electric pressure cooker. Cover baking dish with foil. Fold an 18x12-in. piece of foil lengthwise into thirds to make a sling. Use the sling to lower the dish onto the trivet.
3. Lock lid; close pressure-release valve. Adjust to pressure-cook on high for 20 minutes. Let the pressure release naturally for 10 minutes; quick-release any remaining pressure. Using foil sling, carefully remove baking dish. Let stand 10 minutes. Serve with syrup.
1 serving: 273 cal., 6g fat (2g sat. fat), 100mg chol., 479mg sod., 44g carb. (19g sugars, 1g fiber), 11g pro.

PRESSURE-COOKER SUMMER SQUASH

We love squash, but I got tired of fixing plain old squash and cheese. I decided to jazz it up a bit. This was a huge hit with the family.
—Joan Hallford, North Richland Hills, TX

TAKES: 25 MIN.
MAKES: 8 SERVINGS

- 1 lb. medium yellow summer squash
- 1 lb. medium zucchini
- 2 medium tomatoes, chopped
- 1 cup vegetable broth
- ¼ cup thinly sliced green onions
- ½ tsp. salt
- ¼ tsp. pepper
- 1½ cups Caesar salad croutons, coarsely crushed
- ½ cup shredded cheddar cheese
- 4 bacon strips, cooked and crumbled

1. Cut squash into ¼-in.-thick slices; place in a 6-qt. electric pressure cooker. Add tomatoes, broth, green onions, salt and pepper. Lock lid; close pressure-release valve. Adjust to pressure-cook on high for 1 minute. Quick-release pressure. Remove the squash with a slotted spoon.
2. To serve, top with croutons, cheese and bacon.
¾ cup: 111 cal., 6g fat (2g sat. fat), 12mg chol., 442mg sod., 10g carb. (4g sugars, 1g fiber), 6g pro. **Diabetic exchanges:** 1 vegetable, 1 fat.

AIR-FRYER NASHVILLE HOT CHICKEN

PRESSURE-COOKER SPICY SAUSAGE & BLUE CHEESE PEPPERS

I had an old pressure cooker I inherited from my aunt many years ago before I was married. This was a recipe I had back then and adapted it to my Instant Pot with a few changes. A quick and easy—as well as delicious—meal.
—Joan Hallford, North Richland Hills, TX

PREP: 35 MIN. • **COOK:** 10 MIN.
MAKES: 4 SERVINGS

- 4 large sweet bell peppers
- 1 lb. bulk spicy pork sausage
- 4 green onions, sliced
- 1 garlic clove, minced
- 1 cup cooked brown rice
- ⅓ cup pasta sauce
- 1 tsp. dried oregano
- ¼ tsp. salt
- ¼ tsp. pepper
- 1 cup crumbled blue cheese
- 1 cup beef broth

1. Cut tops from peppers and remove the seeds. Finely chop enough tops to measure ¼ cup for the filling.
2. Select the saute setting on a 6-qt. electric pressure cooker; adjust for medium heat. Cook the sausage, green onions, chopped peppers and garlic until the sausage is no longer pink and the vegetables are tender, 6-8 minutes, breaking up the sausage into crumbles; drain. Press cancel.
3. Stir in rice, pasta sauce, oregano, salt and pepper. Gently stir in blue cheese. Fill peppers with sausage mixture. Wipe pressure cooker clean.
4. Place trivet insert and broth in pressure cooker; place peppers on trivet. Lock lid; close pressure-release valve. Adjust to pressure cook on high for 7 minutes. Quick-release pressure.
1 stuffed pepper: 509 cal., 35g fat (14g sat. fat), 87mg chol., 1,336mg sod., 27g carb. (6g sugars, 5g fiber), 23g pro.

AIR-FRYER NASHVILLE HOT CHICKEN

I live in Tennessee and absolutely love the famous Nashville hot chicken. To make this dish easier and healthier, I tried an air-fryer version. It's almost better than the original!
—April H. Lane, Greeneville, TN

PREP: 30 MIN. • **COOK:** 10 MIN./BATCH
MAKES: 6 SERVINGS

- 2 Tbsp. dill pickle juice, divided
- 2 Tbsp. hot pepper sauce, divided
- 1 tsp. salt, divided
- 2 lbs. chicken tenderloins
- 1 cup all-purpose flour
- ½ tsp. pepper
- 1 large egg
- ½ cup buttermilk
- ½ cup olive oil
- 2 Tbsp. cayenne pepper
- 2 Tbsp. dark brown sugar
- 1 tsp. paprika
- 1 tsp. chili powder
- ½ tsp. garlic powder
  Cooking spray
  Dill pickle slices

1. In a bowl or shallow dish, combine 1 Tbsp. pickle juice, 1 Tbsp. hot sauce and ½ tsp. salt. Add chicken and turn to coat. Refrigerate, covered, at least 1 hour. Drain, discarding any marinade.
2. Preheat air fryer to 375°. In a shallow bowl, mix flour, ½ tsp. salt and pepper. In another shallow bowl, whisk egg, buttermilk, remaining 1 Tbsp. pickle juice and 1 Tbsp. hot sauce. Dip chicken in the flour to coat both sides; shake off excess. Dip in egg mixture, then again in flour mixture.
3. In batches, arrange chicken in a single layer in the generously greased air-fryer basket; spritz the chicken with cooking spray. Cook until the chicken is golden brown, 5-6 minutes. Turn; spritz with cooking spray. Cook until golden brown, 5-6 minutes longer.
4. Whisk together the next 6 ingredients; pour over the hot chicken. Serve with the pickle slices.
5 oz. cooked chicken: 413 cal., 21g fat (3g sat. fat), 96mg chol., 170mg sod., 20g carb. (5g sugars, 1g fiber), 39g pro.

**PRESSURE-COOKER
SPICY SAUSAGE &
BLUE CHEESE PEPPERS**

SUMMER'S ALL-TIME

GRILLED GREATS

You can't mention summer without thinking about the charbroiled favorites everyone craves. From sizzling steaks and juicy burgers to flame-kissed pizzas and seasonal sides, the 14 dishes found here take dining al fresco to new heights.

GINGERED
HONEY
SALMON

GINGERED HONEY SALMON

Ginger, garlic powder and green onion blend nicely in an easy marinade that gives a big flavor boost to salmon. We also like to use this versatile mixture when grilling chicken.
—Dan Strumberger, Farmington, MN

PREP: 10 MIN. + MARINATING
GRILL: 15 MIN. • **MAKES:** 6 SERVINGS

- ⅓ cup orange juice
- ⅓ cup reduced-sodium soy sauce
- ¼ cup honey
- 1 green onion, chopped
- 1 tsp. ground ginger
- 1 tsp. garlic powder
- 1 salmon fillet (1½ lbs. and ¾ in. thick)

1. For marinade, mix first 6 ingredients. In a shallow bowl, combine salmon and ⅔ cup marinade; refrigerate 30 minutes, turning occasionally. Reserve remaining marinade for basting.
2. Place salmon on greased grill rack over medium heat, skin side down; discard marinade remaining in bowl. Grill the salmon, covered, until fish just begins to flake easily with a fork, 15-18 minutes, basting with reserved marinade during the last 5 minutes.
3 oz. cooked fish: 237 cal., 10g fat (2g sat. fat), 57mg chol., 569mg sod., 15g carb. (13g sugars, 0 fiber), 20g pro. **Diabetic exchanges:** 3 lean meat, 1 starch.

Most people think of omega-3s when it comes to salmon, but the fish is also a good source of most B vitamins, which are important to boost energy.

ALL-AMERICAN HAMBURGERS

ALL-AMERICAN HAMBURGERS

We do a lot of camping and outdoor cooking. These hamburgers are on our menu more than any other food.
—Diane Hixon, Niceville, FL

TAKES: 20 MIN. • **MAKES:** 4 SERVINGS

- 1 lb. ground beef
- 2 Tbsp. finely chopped onion
- 2 Tbsp. chili sauce
- 2 tsp. Worcestershire sauce
- 2 tsp. prepared mustard
- 4 slices American cheese or cheddar cheese, halved diagonally
- 2 slices Swiss cheese, halved diagonally
- 4 hamburger buns, split and toasted
  Optional: Lettuce leaves, sliced tomato and onion, cooked bacon strips, ketchup and mustard

1. Combine first 5 ingredients, mixing lightly but thoroughly. Shape mixture into 4 patties. Grill burgers, covered, on a greased rack over medium direct heat until a thermometer reads 160°, about 6 minutes on each side.
2. During the last minute of cooking, top each burger with 2 triangles of American cheese and 1 triangle of Swiss cheese. Serve on the buns; if desired, top with lettuce, tomato, onion, bacon, ketchup or mustard.
1 hamburger: 432 cal., 21g fat (9g sat. fat), 80mg chol., 681mg sod., 26g carb. (6g sugars, 1g fiber), 30g pro.

QUICK BARBECUED BEANS
This is a simple, classic recipe, but cooking it on the grill introduces a subtle flavor. This dish features a nice blend of beans, and the preparation time is minimal.
—Millie Vickery, Lena, IL

TAKES: 25 MIN. • **MAKES:** 5 SERVINGS

- 1 can (16 oz.) kidney beans, rinsed and drained
- 1 can (15½ oz.) great northern beans, rinsed and drained
- 1 can (15 oz.) pork and beans
- ½ cup barbecue sauce
- 2 Tbsp. brown sugar
- 2 tsp. prepared mustard

1. In an ungreased 8-in. square disposable foil pan, combine all of the ingredients.
2. Grill, covered, over medium heat until heated through, 15-20 minutes, carefully stirring occasionally.
¾ cup: 264 cal., 2g fat (0 sat. fat), 0 chol., 877mg sod., 51g carb. (15g sugars, 13g fiber), 14g pro.

SPICED GRILLED CORN
The wonderful spice mixture doesn't add heat—only great flavor. This just may be the best corn you've ever had!
—*Taste of Home* Test Kitchen

TAKES: 20 MIN. • **MAKES:** 8 SERVINGS

- 2 tsp. ground cumin
- 2 tsp. ground coriander
- 1 tsp. salt
- 1 tsp. dried oregano
- ½ tsp. ground ginger
- ¼ tsp. ground cinnamon
- ¼ tsp. pepper
- ⅛ tsp. ground cloves
- 2 Tbsp. olive oil
- 8 medium ears sweet corn, husks removed

1. In a small bowl, combine the first 8 ingredients. Brush oil over the corn; sprinkle with spice mixture. Place each on a piece of heavy-duty foil (about a 14x12-in. rectangle). Fold foil over corn, sealing tightly.
2. Grill corn, covered, over medium heat 10-12 minutes or until tender, turning occasionally. Open foil carefully to allow steam to escape.
1 ear of corn: 113 cal., 5g fat (1g sat. fat), 0 chol., 310mg sod., 18g carb. (3g sugars, 3g fiber), 3g pro. **Diabetic exchanges:** 1 starch, ½ fat.

SWEET GINGER RIBS
People ask what's in the marinade of my glazed ribs with ginger, garlic and peach preserves. Now you know! Psst: It works on steaks and chicken, too.
—Grace McKeone, Schenectady, NY

PREP: 15 MIN. + MARINATING
GRILL: 1½ HOURS • **MAKES:** 8 SERVINGS

- ½ cup soy sauce
- ½ cup red wine vinegar
- ½ cup ketchup
- ½ cup peach preserves
- ⅓ cup minced fresh gingerroot
- 2 Tbsp. stone-ground mustard
- 2 Tbsp. brown sugar
- 6 garlic cloves, minced
- ½ tsp. crushed red pepper flakes
- ½ tsp. coarsely ground pepper
- 4 lbs. pork baby back ribs

1. In a small bowl, whisk the first 10 ingredients until blended. Reserve 1 cup marinade for basting. Divide ribs and the remaining marinade between 2 large resealable containers; seal the containers and turn to coat. Refrigerate ribs and reserved the marinade in the containers overnight.
2. Remove ribs, discarding marinade remaining in the containers. Grill the ribs, covered, over indirect medium heat 1½-2 hours or until tender, basting occasionally with reserved marinade during the last half hour.
1 serving: 338 cal., 21g fat (8g sat. fat), 81mg chol., 721mg sod., 13g carb. (10g sugars, 0 fiber), 24g pro.

HONEY-MUSTARD BRATS

Our honey mustard glaze gives every bite of these brats a sweet and punchy flavor. Everyone who tries them agrees they're simply delicious.
—Lily Julow, Lawrenceville, GA

TAKES: 25 MIN. • **MAKES:** 4 SERVINGS

- ¼ cup Dijon mustard
- ¼ cup honey
- 2 Tbsp. mayonnaise
- 1 tsp. steak sauce
- 4 uncooked bratwurst links
- 4 brat buns, split

1. In a small bowl, mix the mustard, honey, mayonnaise and steak sauce.
2. Grill the bratwurst, covered, over medium heat 15-20 minutes or until a thermometer reads 160°, turning occasionally; brush frequently with the mustard mixture during the last 5 minutes. Serve on buns.
Beer Brats: Cook the bratwurst in 2 cans of simmering beer with a medium onion, halved and sliced, and 2 tsp. fennel seed until a thermometer reads 160°, 7-10 minutes. Grill bratwurst until browned; serve on buns.
1 serving: 624 cal., 35g fat (10g sat. fat), 65mg chol., 1531mg sod., 58g carb. (23g sugars, 1g fiber), 20g pro.

GRILLED POTATO FANS WITH ONIONS

These seasoned potato fans are filled with tender onions, roasted garlic cloves and savory Parmesan cheese. They're my idea of the ultimate grilled potato.
—Sharon Crabtree, Graham, WA

PREP: 20 MIN. • **GRILL:** 35 MIN.
MAKES: 6 SERVINGS

- 6 medium potatoes
- 2 small onions, halved and thinly sliced
- 6 Tbsp. butter, diced
- 2 garlic cloves, minced
- 6 Tbsp. grated Parmesan cheese
- 1 Tbsp. minced chives
- ½ tsp. crushed red pepper flakes
  Dash salt

1. Prepare grill for indirect heat. With a sharp knife, cut each potato into ½-in. slices, leaving the slices attached at the bottom. Fan potatoes slightly. Place each on a 12-in. square of heavy-duty foil.
2. Insert the onions, butter and garlic between potato slices. Combine the cheese, chives, pepper flakes and salt; sprinkle between slices. Fold foil around potatoes and seal tightly.
3. Grill, covered, over indirect medium heat for 35-45 minutes or until tender. Open foil carefully to allow steam to escape.
1 potato: 302 cal., 13g fat (8g sat. fat), 35mg chol., 195mg sod., 41g carb. (4g sugars, 4g fiber), 7g pro.

GRILLED CAPRESE QUESADILLAS

This is a quick and healthy summer recipe with ingredients right from the backyard garden. Feta or goat cheese can be used instead of the mozzarella cheese, or add some grilled chicken.
—Amy Mongiovi, Lititz, PA

TAKES: 20 MIN. • **MAKES:** 2 SERVINGS

- 4 whole wheat tortillas (8 in.)
- 6 oz. fresh mozzarella cheese, sliced
- 2 medium tomatoes, sliced and patted dry
- ⅓ cup julienned fresh basil
- ¼ cup pitted Greek olives, chopped
  Freshly ground pepper to taste

1. Layer 1 half of each tortilla with cheese and tomatoes; sprinkle with basil, olives and pepper to taste. Fold tortillas to close.
2. Grill, covered, over medium-high heat until lightly browned and the cheese is melted, 2-3 minutes per side.
1 serving: 535 cal., 25g fat (13g sat. fat), 67mg chol., 665mg sod., 52g carb. (5g sugars, 8g fiber), 25g pro.

GRILLED APPLE TOSSED SALAD

GRILLED CHICKEN, MANGO & BLUE CHEESE TORTILLAS

Tortillas packed with chicken, mango and blue cheese make a fantastic appetizer to welcome summer. We double or triple the ingredients when we host parties.
—Josee Lanzi, New Port Richey, FL

TAKES: 30 MIN. • **MAKES:** 16 APPETIZERS

- 1   boneless skinless chicken breast (8 oz.)
- 1   tsp. blackened seasoning
- ¾   cup plain yogurt
- 1½   tsp. grated lime zest
- 2   Tbsp. lime juice
- ¼   tsp. salt
- ⅛   tsp. pepper
- 1   cup finely chopped peeled mango
- ⅓   cup finely chopped red onion
- 4   flour tortillas (8 in.)
- ½   cup crumbled blue cheese
- 2   Tbsp. minced fresh cilantro

1. Lightly coat grill rack with cooking oil. Sprinkle chicken with blackened seasoning. Grill chicken, covered, over medium heat 6-8 minutes on each side or until a thermometer reads 165°.
2. Meanwhile, in a small bowl, mix the yogurt, lime zest, lime juice, salt and pepper. Cool chicken slightly; finely chop and transfer to a small bowl. Stir in the mango and onion.
3. Grill tortillas, uncovered, over medium heat 2-3 minutes or until they puff. Turn; top with the chicken mixture and blue cheese. Grill, covered, 2-3 minutes longer or until bottoms of tortillas are lightly browned. Drizzle with the yogurt mixture; sprinkle with cilantro. Cut each tortilla into 4 wedges.
1 wedge: 85 cal., 3g fat (1g sat. fat), 12mg chol., 165mg sod., 10g carb. (2g sugars, 1g fiber), 5g pro. **Diabetic exchanges:** 1 lean meat, ½ starch.

→

Serve these open-faced appetizers as a colorful lunch or a light dinner alongside a green salad and white rice.

GRILLED APPLE TOSSED SALAD

The grilled apples in this salad combine so well with the blue cheese, walnuts and balsamic dressing. I like to serve it on pink Depression glass dessert plates from my great-grandmother.
—Paul Soska, Toledo, OH

PREP: 15 MIN. + MARINATING
GRILL: 10 MIN. • **MAKES:** 6 SERVINGS

- 6   Tbsp. olive oil
- ¼   cup minced fresh cilantro
- ¼   cup orange juice
- ¼   cup white or regular balsamic vinegar
- 2   Tbsp. honey
- 1   garlic clove, minced
- ½   tsp. salt
- ½   tsp. Sriracha chili sauce
- 2   large apples, cut into ½-in. wedges
- 1   pkg. (5 oz.) spring mix salad greens
- 1   cup walnut halves, toasted
- ½   cup crumbled blue cheese

1. For dressing, whisk together the first 8 ingredients. In a bowl, toss apples with ¼ cup dressing. Let stand 10 minutes.
2. Place apple slices on a grill rack over medium heat; reserve dressing left in bowl. Grill apples, covered, until tender and lightly browned, 3-4 minutes per side, brushing with reserved marinade.
3. To serve, toss greens with remaining dressing. Top with the grilled apples, walnuts and cheese.
Note: To toast nuts, bake in a shallow pan in a 350° oven for 5-10 minutes or cook in a skillet over low heat until lightly browned, stirring occasionally.
1 serving: 341 cal., 28g fat (5g sat. fat), 8mg chol., 360mg sod., 22g carb. (16g sugars, 3g fiber), 6g pro.
Health tip: Lighten this salad by leaving off the walnuts and blue cheese. You'll save 150 calories per serving, but the grilled apples and homemade dressing will still make it taste like it came from a restaurant.

GRILLED CHICKEN,
MANGO & BLUE CHEESE
TORTILLAS

CAJUN GRILLED SHRIMP

The kicked-up marinade on these shrimp makes this a flavor-packed dish. Serve over some rice, and make sure to squeeze the charred lemons over the top—that makes the shrimp taste extra light and delicious.
—Sharon Delaney-Chronis, South Milwaukee, WI

TAKES: 30 MIN. • **MAKES:** 6 SERVINGS

- 3 green onions, finely chopped
- 2 Tbsp. lemon juice
- 1 Tbsp. olive oil
- 3 garlic cloves, minced
- 2 tsp. paprika
- 1 tsp. salt
- ¼ tsp. pepper
- ¼ tsp. cayenne pepper
- 2 lbs. uncooked medium shrimp, peeled and deveined with tails on
- 4 medium lemons, each cut into 8 wedges

1. In a large resealable container, combine the first 8 ingredients. Add the shrimp; seal container and turn to coat. Refrigerate for 15 minutes.
2. Drain shrimp, discarding marinade. On each of 12 metal or soaked wooden skewers, thread the shrimp and the lemon wedges.
3. Grill, covered, over medium heat or broil 4 in. from the heat until shrimp turn pink, turning once, 6-8 minutes.
2 skewers: 168 cal., 5g fat (1g sat. fat), 184mg chol., 575mg sod., 7g carb. (1g sugars, 2g fiber), 25g pro. **Diabetic exchanges:** 3 lean meat, ½ fruit, ½ fat.

GRILLED CHICKEN RANCH BURGERS

GRILLED CHICKEN RANCH BURGERS

This is one of the most fantastic, flavorful burgers I've ever made. Ranch flavor is a favorite in dips and dressings, and believe me, it doesn't disappoint in these tasty burgers, either!
—Kari Shifflett, Lake Mills, IA

PREP: 15 MIN. + CHILLING
GRILL: 10 MIN.
MAKES: 16 SERVINGS

- ¾ cup ranch salad dressing
- ¾ cup panko bread crumbs
- ¾ cup grated Parmesan cheese
- 3 Tbsp. Worcestershire sauce
- 3 garlic cloves, minced
- 3 tsp. pepper
- 4 lbs. ground chicken
- 3 Tbsp. olive oil
- 16 hamburger buns, split
  Optional toppings: Tomato slices, lettuce leaves, sliced red onion, sliced cucumber, sliced avocado and ranch dip

1. In a large bowl, mix first 6 ingredients. Add chicken; mix lightly but thoroughly. Shape mixture into sixteen ½-in. thick patties. Brush both sides of patties with oil; refrigerate, covered, 15 minutes to allow patties to firm up.
2. Grill the burgers, covered, over medium heat or broil 3-4 in. from heat 5-6 minutes on each side or until a thermometer reads 165°. Serve on buns with desired toppings.
1 burger: 371 cal., 19g fat (5g sat. fat), 79mg chol., 498mg sod., 26g carb. (4g sugars, 1g fiber), 24g pro.

STACK IT UP!

The recipe for Grilled Chicken Ranch Burgers is easy to halve and even easier to customize. Consider these toppings to amp up the flavor.

- Buffalo wing sauce
- Cooked bacon
- Cucumber slices
- Sharp cheddar cheese
- Yellow pepper strips
- Pickle chips
- Fig jam
- Barbecue sauce
- Swiss cheese

GRILLED MARINATED RIBEYES

GRILLED MARINATED RIBEYES

These juicy steaks are a favorite meal of ours when we go camping. Let them sit in a tangy, barbecue-inspired marinade overnight and you've got a rich and hearty dinner ready to grill up the next day.
—Louise Graybiel, Toronto, ON

PREP: 10 MIN. + MARINATING
GRILL: 10 MIN. • **MAKES:** 4 SERVINGS

- ½ cup barbecue sauce
- 3 Tbsp. Worcestershire sauce
- 3 Tbsp. olive oil
- 2 Tbsp. steak sauce
- 1 Tbsp. red wine vinegar
- 1 Tbsp. reduced-sodium soy sauce
- 2 tsp. steak seasoning
- 1 tsp. hot pepper sauce
- 1 garlic clove, minced
- 4 beef ribeye steaks (8 oz. each)

1. In a large resealable container, mix first 9 ingredients. Add steaks; seal container and turn to coat. Refrigerate 4 hours or overnight.

2. Drain steaks, discarding marinade. Grill steaks, covered, over medium heat until meat reaches desired doneness (for medium-rare, a thermometer should read 135°; medium, 140°), 5-7 minutes per side.

Freeze option: Freeze steaks with the marinade in a resealable freezer container. To use, thaw in refrigerator overnight. Drain beef, discarding marinade. Grill as directed.

1 steak: 570 cal., 40g fat (15g sat. fat), 134mg chol., 592mg sod., 8g carb. (6g sugars, 0 fiber), 40g pro.

Ribeyes are a favorite choice for grilling, but leaner cuts work with this marinade, too. Think top sirloin, top loin (aka strip), flank and top blade (aka flat iron) steaks.

GRILLED SWEET POTATOES WITH GORGONZOLA SPREAD

My husband first tried this recipe with plain potatoes. They were so yummy; we experimented with sweet potatoes. Dipped in Gorgonzola spread, they're irresistible.
—Kristen Minello, Macomb, MI

PREP: 25 MIN. • **GRILL:** 10 MIN.
MAKES: 8 SERVINGS

- 4 large sweet potatoes
- 1 cup (4 oz.) crumbled Gorgonzola cheese
- ½ cup mayonnaise
- 1 to 2 Tbsp. lemon juice
- 3 Tbsp. olive oil
- ½ tsp. salt
- ¼ tsp. pepper
  Minced chives, optional

1. Scrub sweet potatoes and pierce them with a fork; place on a microwave-safe plate. Microwave, uncovered, on high just until tender, turning potatoes once, 6-8 minutes.

2. Meanwhile, in a small bowl, combine cheese, mayonnaise and lemon juice. Refrigerate until serving.

3. Slice potatoes into ½-in.-thick rounds; brush both sides with oil. Sprinkle with salt and pepper. Grill, covered, over medium heat or broil 4 in. from heat on each side until browned, 4-5 minutes. Serve with spread. If desired, sprinkle with chives.

1 serving with 3 Tbsp. spread: 362 cal., 19g fat (5g sat. fat), 14mg chol., 425mg sod., 42g carb. (17g sugars, 6g fiber), 6g pro.

SUMMER'S HOTTEST

CELEBRATIONS

Friends, family, fresh air and fantastic foods are what summer is all about. Whether you celebrate the season with backyard barbecues, delightful brunches or campfire feasts, the four menus that follow make summer entertaining deliciously easy.

BACKYARD
BBQ BASH

CLEO'S
POTATO
SALAD

5i
LEMONY PINEAPPLE ICED TEA
I like to garnish this iced tea with some of our sweet Hawaiian pineapple.
—Beverly Toomey, Honolulu, HI

PREP: 20 MIN. + CHILLING • **COOK:** 10 MIN.
MAKES: 20 SERVINGS

- 16 cups water
- 24 tea bags
- 6 fresh mint sprigs
- 3⅓ cups sugar
- 3 cups unsweetened pineapple juice
- 1 cup lemon juice

1. In a stockpot, bring water to boil; remove from heat. Add tea bags; steep, covered, 10 minutes. Discard tea bags. Add mint; steep 5 minutes; discard mint. Add remaining ingredients, stirring to dissolve sugar.
2. Transfer to pitchers or a large covered container. Refrigerate, covered, until cold. If desired, serve with ice.
1 cup: 154 cal., 0 fat (0 sat. fat), 0 chol., 7mg sod., 40g carb. (38g sugars, 0 fiber), 0 pro.

CLEO'S POTATO SALAD
My mom, Cleo Lightfoot, loved cooking all kinds of recipes, but her favorite meal was one she made when she hosted backyard barbecues in the summer. She would make her famous ribs, baked beans and this delicious potato salad.
—Joan Hallford, North Richland Hills, TX

PREP: 25 MIN. • **COOK:** 20 MIN.
MAKES: 12 SERVINGS

- 3½ lbs. red potatoes (about 12 medium), cut into 1-in. cubes
- 6 bacon strips, chopped
- ¼ cup sugar
- 1 Tbsp. all-purpose flour
- ½ cup water
- 1 large egg, lightly beaten
- 3 Tbsp. cider vinegar
- 1 Tbsp. grated onion
- 1 tsp. celery seed
- 1 tsp. salt
- ½ tsp. pepper
- 1 cup heavy whipping cream, whipped
- 4 hard-boiled large eggs, chopped
- 2 medium celery ribs, chopped

1. Place potatoes in a large saucepan; cover with water. Bring to a boil. Reduce the heat; cook, uncovered, until tender, 10-15 minutes. Drain; cool completely.
2. Meanwhile, in a saucepan, cook the bacon over medium heat until crisp. Remove bacon with a slotted spoon; drain on paper towels. Remove all but 1 Tbsp. drippings from pan.
3. Stir sugar and flour into drippings until smooth. Gradually stir in water; cook and stir over medium-high heat until thickened and bubbly. Remove from heat. Stir a small amount of hot mixture into beaten egg; return all to pan, stirring constantly. Slowly bring to a boil, stirring constantly; remove from heat. Transfer to a large bowl; cool completely.
4. Gently stir in the vinegar, onion and seasonings. Fold in whipped cream. Stir in eggs, celery, potatoes and bacon. Refrigerate, covered, until serving.
¾ cup: 211 cal., 11g fat (5g sat. fat), 90mg chol., 272mg sod., 23g carb. (5g sugars, 2g fiber), 6g pro.

MELON-BERRY SALAD

The best way to cool down on a warm day is to serve up a chilled fruit salad—the best of summer's bounty! The dressing gives this salad a creamy and rich texture, and the coconut milk makes it even more decadent. This can be served at breakfast, brunch or as a dessert! Wait until just before serving to garnish the salad, otherwise the toasted coconut will get soggy.
—Carrie Hirsch, Hilton Head Island, SC

TAKES: 20 MIN. • **MAKES:** 12 SERVINGS

- 1 cup fat-free vanilla Greek yogurt
- ½ cup coconut milk
- ½ cup orange juice
- 4 cups cubed cantaloupe (½-in.)
- 4 cups cubed watermelon (½-in.)
- 2 medium navel oranges, sectioned
- 1 cup fresh raspberries
- 1 cup fresh blueberries
- ½ cup sweetened shredded coconut, toasted

1. For the dressing, whisk together the yogurt, coconut milk and orange juice. Refrigerate until serving.
2. To serve, place fruit in a large bowl; toss gently with dressing. Sprinkle with the coconut.
Note: To toast coconut, bake in a shallow pan in a 350° oven for 5-10 minutes or cook in a skillet over low heat until golden brown, stirring occasionally.
¾ cup: 105 cal., 3g fat (3g sat. fat), 0 chol., 30mg sod., 19g carb. (16g sugars, 2g fiber), 3g pro. **Diabetic exchanges:** 1 fruit, ½ fat.

SHRIMP TOSTADAS WITH LIME-CILANTRO SAUCE

SHRIMP TOSTADAS WITH LIME-CILANTRO SAUCE

I love shrimp and veggies marinated in citrus juice—also known as ceviche. This recipe starts with cooked shrimp and those same fresh ceviche flavors. Enjoy these tostadas as a make-ahead appetizer or dinner entree.
—Leslie Kelley, Dorris, CA

PREP: 35 MIN. + STANDING
MAKES: 10 SERVINGS

- 1½ lbs. peeled and deveined cooked shrimp (26-30 per lb.), coarsely chopped
- 1½ cups chopped, peeled English cucumber
- 8 radishes, thinly sliced
- 4 plum tomatoes, chopped
- 4 green onions, chopped
- 2 jalapeno peppers, seeded and minced
- 2 Tbsp. minced fresh cilantro
- 2 Tbsp. lime juice
- 3 garlic cloves, minced
- 1 tsp. salt
- ¼ tsp. pepper
- 1 medium ripe avocado, peeled and cubed

SAUCE
- 1 cup sour cream
- 2 Tbsp. minced fresh cilantro
- 1 tsp. grated lime zest
- 1 Tbsp. lime juice
- ¼ tsp. salt
- ¼ tsp. ground cumin
- ⅛ tsp. pepper

ASSEMBLY
- 10 tostada shells

1. Place first 11 ingredients in a large bowl; toss to combine. Gently stir in the avocado; let stand 15 minutes.
2. In a small bowl, mix sauce ingredients. To serve, spread the tostada shells with sauce. Top with shrimp mixture.
1 tostada: 209 cal., 12g fat (4g sat. fat), 109mg chol., 448mg sod., 12g carb. (3g sugars, 2g fiber), 16g pro.

the tip of a pastry bag; insert a 1M star tip. Fill with cream mixture; pipe rosettes over pie. Sprinkle with the hazelnuts. Top with chocolate decorations.

Note: Let pie weights cool before storing. Beans and rice may be reused for pie weights, but not for cooking.

1 piece: 578 cal., 46g fat (24g sat. fat), 107mg chol., 147mg sod., 39g carb. (22g sugars, 2g fiber), 7g pro.

SPICED PULLED PORK SANDWICHES

PICTURED ON PAGE 70

This pulled pork is tender and has a fabulous spice rub. It's my sweetie's favorite meal, and I love that it is so easy. You may add more or less salt to taste.

—Katie Citrowske, Bozeman, MT

PREP: 30 MIN. • **COOK:** 6 HOURS
MAKES: 10 SERVINGS

- 1½ tsp. salt
- 1½ tsp. garlic powder
- 1½ tsp. ground cumin
- 1½ tsp. ground cinnamon
- 1½ tsp. chili powder
- 1½ tsp. coarsely ground pepper
- 1 boneless pork shoulder butt roast (3 to 4 lbs.), halved
- 2 Tbsp. olive oil
- 2 medium onions, halved and sliced
- 8 garlic cloves, coarsely chopped
- 1½ cups water
- 1 Tbsp. liquid smoke, optional
- 10 hamburger buns, split and toasted
   Barbecue sauce
   Sliced jalapeno pepper, optional

1. Mix seasonings; rub over pork. In large skillet, heat oil over medium heat. Brown pork on all sides. Transfer to a 5- or 6-qt. slow cooker.

2. In same pan, cook and stir onions over medium heat until lightly browned, 4-5 minutes. Add garlic; cook and stir 1 minute. Add water; bring to a boil, stirring to loosen browned bits from pan. If desired, stir in liquid smoke. Add to pork.

3. Cook, covered, on low until meat is tender, 6-8 hours. Remove roast; discard onion mixture. Shred pork with 2 forks; return to slow cooker and heat through. Serve on buns with barbecue sauce and, if desired, jalapeno slices.

1 sandwich: 386 cal., 18g fat (6g sat. fat), 81mg chol., 669mg sod., 26g carb. (4g sugars, 2g fiber), 28g pro.

NUTELLA BANANA CREAM PIE

NUTELLA BANANA CREAM PIE

Here's a banana cream pie with Italian flair. The chocolate and hazelnut go well with the banana, and the rolled chocolate pie crust makes it extra special. If you don't have time to melt and pipe the chocolate stars, just sprinkle the top of the pie with grated chocolate or cocoa powder instead.

—Crystal Schlueter, Northglenn, MN

PREP: 45 MIN. + CHILLING
BAKE: 20 MIN. + COOLING
MAKES: 10 SERVINGS

- 1¼ cups all-purpose flour
- 2 Tbsp. baking cocoa
- 1 Tbsp. sugar
- ½ cup cold butter, cubed
- 3 to 4 Tbsp. cold brewed coffee

DECORATIONS
- ¼ cup semisweet chocolate chips
- ¼ tsp. shortening

FILLING
- 1 carton (8 oz.) mascarpone cheese
- ¾ cup Nutella
- 2 medium bananas, thinly sliced
- 2 cups heavy whipping cream
- 3 Tbsp. instant banana cream pudding mix
- 2 Tbsp. chopped hazelnuts, toasted

1. In a small bowl, mix the flour, cocoa and sugar; cut in butter until crumbly. Gradually add cold coffee, tossing with a fork until dough holds together when pressed. Shape into a disk; wrap and refrigerate 1 hour or overnight.

2. On a lightly floured surface, roll dough to a ⅛-in.-thick circle; transfer to a 9-in. pie plate. Trim the crust to ½ in. beyond rim of plate; flute the edge. Refrigerate 30 minutes. Preheat oven to 425°.

3. Line crust with a double thickness of foil. Fill with pie weights, dried beans or uncooked rice. Bake on a lower oven rack until set, 15-20 minutes. Remove foil and weights; bake until the edge are browned, about 5 minutes. Cool completely on a wire rack.

4. For decorations, in a microwave, melt chocolate chips and shortening; stir until smooth. Transfer to a pastry bag with a small round tip. Pipe the star designs over a waxed paper-lined baking sheet. Freeze until set, about 5 minutes.

5. For filling, mix mascarpone cheese and Nutella until blended; spread into crust. Top with bananas.

6. In another bowl, beat cream until it begins to thicken. Add pudding mix; beat until stiff peaks form. Cut a small hole in

WARM-WEATHER BRUNCH

LIME-RASPBERRY PIE
WITH COCONUT CREAM

LIME-RASPBERRY PIE WITH COCONUT CREAM

On my family trips to Florida, I've had Key lime pie from many restaurants, and each one is different. I wanted to create my own spin on the pie to make it my signature dessert. Whipped egg whites in the filling make it light and mousse-like, sweet raspberries balance the tart filling, and coconut and cashews add tropical flair. Garnish with raspberries and toasted flaked coconut if desired.
—Elise Easterling, Chapel Hill, NC

PREP: 50 MIN. • **BAKE:** 25 MIN. + CHILLING
MAKES: 12 SERVINGS

- 3 large egg whites
- 18 whole graham crackers, crushed (about 2½ cups)
- ½ cup packed brown sugar
- ½ cup unsalted cashews, finely chopped
- ¾ cup butter, melted
- 2 cans (14 oz. each) sweetened condensed milk
- ¾ cup Key lime juice
- 6 large egg yolks
- ¼ cup sugar

TOPPINGS
- 1 can (13.66 oz.) coconut milk
- 1 cup heavy whipping cream
- ½ cup confectioners' sugar
- ½ cup seedless raspberry jam
  Optional: Fresh raspberries and toasted flaked coconut

1. Place egg whites in a small bowl; let stand at room temperature 30 minutes. Preheat oven to 350°.
2. In a large bowl, mix crushed crackers, brown sugar and cashews; stir in melted butter. Press onto bottom and 2 in. up side of a greased 9-in. springform pan.
3. In a large bowl, mix condensed milk, lime juice and egg yolks until blended. In another bowl, with clean beaters, beat egg whites on medium speed until soft peaks form. Gradually add sugar, 1 Tbsp. at a time, beating mixture on high after each addition until the sugar is dissolved. Continue beating until stiff peaks form. Fold into milk mixture; pour into crust.
4. Bake 25-30 minutes or until filling is set. Cool 4 hours on a wire rack. Refrigerate 6 hours or overnight, covering only after the pie is cold.
5. Spoon the cream layer from top of coconut milk into a large bowl (discard remaining liquid). Add whipping cream and confectioners' sugar to bowl; beat until stiff peaks form.
6. Spread jam over pie. If desired, top with raspberries and coconut. Serve with coconut cream.
Note: To toast coconut, bake in a shallow pan in a 350° oven for 5-10 minutes or cook in a skillet over low heat until it is golden brown, stirring occasionally. Light coconut milk is not recommended for this recipe.
1 piece: 678 cal., 34g fat (20g sat. fat), 168mg chol., 349mg sod., 86g carb. (69 sugars, 1g fiber), 11g pro.

CHAMPAGNE SIPPER

This is a terrific cocktail for a holiday celebration. And because you make it by the pitcher, you can mingle with your guests instead of tending bar.
—Moffat Frazier, New York, NY

TAKES: 10 MIN. • **MAKES:** 12 SERVINGS

- 1½ cups sugar
- 1 cup lemon juice
- 3 cups cold water
- 1½ cups sweet white wine, chilled
- 1 bottle (750 ml) champagne, chilled
  Sliced fresh strawberries, optional

In a 3-qt. pitcher, dissolve sugar in lemon juice. Add the cold water and wine. Stir in champagne. If desired, serve sipper with strawberries.
¾ cup: 162 cal., 11g fat (5g sat. fat), 49mg chol., 323mg sod., 1g carb. (0 sugars, 0 fiber), 13g pro.

STRAWBERRY & CREAM BRUSCHETTA

This is a dessert take on bruschetta. Sweet, cinnamony toast slices are topped with a cream cheese mixture, strawberries and almonds. They taste like mini cheesecakes!
—Christi Meixner, Aurora, IL

TAKES: 25 MIN. • **MAKES:** 2 DOZEN

- 1   French bread baguette (8 oz.), cut into 24 slices
- ¼   cup butter, melted
- 3   Tbsp. sugar
- ½   tsp. ground cinnamon
- 1   pkg. (8 oz.) cream cheese, softened
- ¼   cup confectioners' sugar
- 2   tsp. lemon juice
- 1   tsp. grated lemon zest
- 2½ cups fresh strawberries, chopped
- ⅓   cup slivered almonds, toasted

1. Preheat oven to 375°. Place bread on an ungreased baking sheet; brush with butter. Combine sugar and cinnamon; sprinkle over bread. Bake 4-5 minutes on each side or until lightly crisp.
2. In a small bowl, beat cream cheese, confectioners' sugar, lemon juice and zest until blended; spread over toast. Top with strawberries; sprinkle with slivered almonds.
1 appetizer: 94 cal., 6g fat (3g sat. fat), 15mg chol., 70mg sod., 8g carb. (4g sugars, 1g fiber), 2g pro.

HOMEMADE SAGE
SAUSAGE PATTIES

HOMEMADE SAGE SAUSAGE PATTIES

Oregano, garlic and sage add savory flavor to these quick-to-fix ground pork patties. I've had this Pennsylvania Dutch recipe for years, and it always brings compliments.
—Diane Hixon, Niceville, FL

PREP: 10 MIN. + CHILLING • **COOK:** 15 MIN.
MAKES: 8 SERVINGS

- 1   lb. ground pork
- ¾   cup shredded cheddar cheese
- ¼   cup buttermilk
- 1   Tbsp. finely chopped onion
- 2   tsp. rubbed sage
- ¾   tsp. salt
- ¾   tsp. pepper
- ⅛   tsp. garlic powder
- ⅛   tsp. dried oregano

1. In a bowl, combine all the ingredients, mixing lightly but thoroughly. Shape into eight ½-in.-thick patties. Refrigerate 1 hour.
2. In a large cast-iron or other heavy skillet, cook the patties over medium heat until a thermometer reads 160° 6-8 minutes on each side.
1 patty: 162 cal., 11g fat (5g sat. fat), 49mg chol., 323mg sod., 1g carb. (0 sugars, 0 fiber), 13g pro.

Wrap the cooked and cooled patties in foil and store them all in a freezer storage bag. This makes it a snap to grab one or two to heat up on particularly busy mornings.

ARTICHOKE & ONION FRITTATA

CRAB CAKE LETTUCE WRAPS

I love dishes that you can put together quickly and eat with your hands. These little crab wraps are healthy, fast and flavorful.
—Joyce Huang, New York, NY

TAKES: 10 MIN. • **MAKES:** 1 DOZEN

- 2 cans (6 oz. each) lump crabmeat, drained
- ¼ cup finely chopped celery
- ¼ cup seasoned stuffing cubes, coarsely crushed
- ¼ cup plain Greek yogurt
- ⅛ tsp. salt
- ⅛ tsp. pepper
- 12 Bibb or Boston lettuce leaves
   Finely chopped tomatoes, optional

In a large bowl, mix crab, celery, stuffing cubes, yogurt, salt and pepper. To serve, spoon 2 Tbsp. crab mixture into each lettuce leaf. If desired, sprinkle with tomatoes. Fold lettuce over filling.

1 filled lettuce wrap: 37 cal., 0 fat (0 sat. fat), 25mg chol., 139mg sod., 1g carb. (0 sugars, 0 fiber), 7g pro.

ARTICHOKE & ONION FRITTATA

The combination of fresh flavors make this pretty egg bake a great entree for a special-occasion brunch or even a light luncheon with friends..
—Joyce Moynihan, Lakeville, MN

PREP: 15 MIN. • **BAKE:** 35 MIN.
MAKES: 8 SERVINGS

- 1 pkg. (8 oz.) frozen artichoke hearts
- 1 Tbsp. butter
- 1 Tbsp. olive oil
- 1 medium onion, chopped
- 1 garlic clove, minced
- ¼ tsp. dried oregano
- ¾ cup shredded Parmesan cheese, divided
- 6 large eggs
- ½ cup 2% milk
- ¼ tsp. salt
- ⅛ tsp. white pepper
- ⅛ tsp. ground nutmeg
- 1 cup shredded Monterey Jack cheese
   Minced chives, optional

1. Cook artichokes according to package directions; drain. Cool slightly; coarsely chop. Preheat oven to 350°.
2. In a large skillet, heat butter and oil over medium-high heat. Add onion; cook and stir until tender. Add garlic; cook 1 minute longer. Stir in oregano and artichokes; remove from heat.
3. Sprinkle ¼ cup Parmesan cheese in a greased 11x7-in. baking dish. Top with artichoke mixture.
4. In a large bowl, whisk the eggs, milk, salt, pepper and nutmeg. Stir in Monterey Jack cheese and ¼ cup Parmesan cheese. Pour over the artichoke mixture.
5. Bake, uncovered, 30 minutes. Sprinkle with the remaining Parmesan cheese. Bake 6-8 minutes longer or until a knife inserted in the center comes out clean. If desired, sprinkle with minced chives.
1 serving: 192 cal., 13g fat (7g sat. fat), 163mg chol., 373mg sod., 5g carb. (2 sugars, 2g fiber), 13g pro.

CAMPFIRE CLASSICS

BONFIRE
COOKIES

ZUCCHINI & SUMMER SQUASH SALAD

I came up with this colorful and tasty salad years ago for a recipe contest. I was delighted when I won an honorable mention! The recipe easily doubles and is the perfect dish to take to potlucks or family gatherings.
—Paula Wharton, El Paso, TX

PREP: 25 MIN. + CHILLING
MAKES: 12 SERVINGS

- 4 medium zucchini
- 2 yellow summer squash
- 1 medium sweet red pepper
- 1 medium red onion
- 1 cup fresh sugar snap peas, trimmed and halved
- ⅓ cup olive oil
- ¼ cup balsamic vinegar
- 2 Tbsp. reduced-fat mayonnaise
- 4 tsp. fresh sage or 1 tsp. dried sage leaves
- 2 tsp. honey
- 1 tsp. garlic powder
- 1 tsp. celery seed
- 1 tsp. dill weed
- ½ tsp. salt
- ½ tsp. pepper

Thinly slice zucchini, squash, red pepper and onion; place in a large bowl. Add the snap peas. In a small bowl, whisk the remaining ingredients until blended. Pour over the vegetables; toss to coat. Refrigerate, covered, at least 3 hours.

¾ cup: 101 cal., 7g fat (1g sat. fat), 1mg chol., 124mg sod., 8g carb. (6g sugars, 2g fiber, 2g pro.

BONFIRE COOKIES

When it's bonfire weather in Colorado, I like to celebrate with these clever cookies!
—Callie Washer, Conifer, CO

PREP: 45 MIN.
BAKE: 10 MIN./BATCH + COOLING
MAKES: 2 DOZEN

- 1 cup butter, softened
- 1½ cups sugar
- 2 large eggs, room temperature
- 1 tsp. vanilla extract
- 3 cups all-purpose flour
- 1½ tsp. baking powder
- ¼ tsp. salt
- ¼ tsp. ground nutmeg
- 10 cherry Jolly Rancher hard candies, crushed
- 1 pouch (7 oz.) green decorating icing
- ½ cup chocolate wafer crumbs
- 36 pretzel sticks

1. Preheat the oven to 350°. In a large bowl, cream the butter and sugar until light and fluffy, 5-7 minutes. Beat in eggs and vanilla. In another bowl, whisk the flour, baking powder, salt and nutmeg; gradually beat into creamed mixture.

2. Shape level tablespoons of dough into balls; place 2 in. apart on ungreased baking sheets. Flatten slightly with the bottom of a glass. Bake until edges are light brown, 8-10 minutes. Cool on pans 2 minutes before removing to wire racks to cool completely.

3. Meanwhile, spread crushed candies onto a parchment-lined baking sheet. Bake until candy is melted, 5-7 minutes. Cool completely on pan on a wire rack. Break into pieces.

4. Spread icing over cookies; sprinkle with wafer crumbs. Arrange the candy pieces to make campfire flames. For logs, break pretzel sticks in half. Place 3 halves, broken edges down, in the wet icing. Hold in place until set.

1 cookie: 238 cal., 10g fat (6g sat. fat), 36mg chol., 166mg sod., 35g carb. (20g sugars, 1g fiber), 2g pro.

If the bottom of the glass sticks to the dough, simply dip it in a little flour before flattening the balls into the cookie rounds.

SAUSAGE & POTATO CAMPFIRE PACKETS

PICTURED ON PAGE 78

My family enjoys camping and cooking over a fire. These easy packets turn out beautifully over a campfire, on the grill or in the oven at home. We sometimes leave out the sausage and serve the potatoes as a side dish. Either way, it's so easy—and the spuds can be served right from the foil pouch for easy cleanup. The recipe also tastes amazing when cooked in a Dutch oven.
—Julie Koets, Elkhart, IN

PREP: 20 MIN. • **COOK:** 30 MIN.
MAKES: 8 SERVINGS

- 3 lbs. red potatoes, cut into ½-in. cubes
- 2 pkg. (12 oz. each) smoked sausage links, cut into ½-in. slices
- 4 bacon strips, cooked and crumbled
- 1 medium onion, chopped
- 2 Tbsp. chopped fresh parsley
- ¼ tsp. salt
- ¼ tsp. garlic salt
- ¼ tsp. pepper
   Additional chopped fresh parsley, optional

1. Prepare campfire or grill for medium heat. In a large bowl, toss the potatoes with the sausage, bacon, onion, parsley, salts and pepper.
2. Divide mixture among eight 18x12-in. pieces of heavy-duty nonstick foil, placing food on dull side of foil. Fold foil around potato mixture, sealing tightly.
3. Place packets over campfire or grill; cook 15 minutes on each side or until potatoes are tender. Open the packets carefully to allow steam to escape. If desired, sprinkle with additional parsley.
1 packet: 414 cal., 25g fat (10g sat. fat), 61mg chol., 1,181mg sod., 31g carb. (4g sugars, 3g fiber), 17g pro.

CAMPFIRE DESSERT CONES

CAMPFIRE DESSERT CONES

Kids love to make these sweet treats! Set out the ingredients so they can mix and match their own creations.
—Bonnie Hawkins, Elkhorn, WI

TAKES: 20 MIN. • **MAKES:** 8 SERVINGS

- 8 ice cream sugar cones
- ½ cup milk chocolate M&M's
- ½ cup miniature marshmallows
- ½ cup salted peanuts
- ½ cup white baking chips

1. Prepare the campfire or grill for medium heat. Fill cones with M&M's, marshmallows, peanuts and white chips. Fully wrap each cone with foil, sealing tightly.
2. Place packets over campfire or grill; cook until heated through, 7-10 minutes. Open foil carefully.
1 cone: 217 cal., 11g fat (5g sat. fat), 4mg chol., 78mg sod., 26g carb. (18g sugars, 1g fiber), 5g pro.

COOKING UP CAMP CHOW

One of the best parts about camping? Eating around the fire!

If you have a fire pit in your backyard, it's easy to roast hot dogs, toast marshmallows, and even cook up meats and veggies in foil packets.

If you don't have a fire pit, a small charcoal grill works well for many foods. You can make pudgy pies over the coals whenever tummies start to grumble.

But you don't necessarily need a campfire to eat like a camper. Pack sandwiches, whole fruit, trail mix, juice boxes and desserts in a cooler to have at the ready.

PINEAPPLE UPSIDE-DOWN CAMPFIRE CAKE

We make this fun recipe while camping or in the backyard around a fire. Kids love it, but the sandwich iron should be opened only by adults to avoid burns.

—Cheryl Grimes, Whiteland, IN

PREP: 10 MIN. • **COOK:** 5 MIN./CAKE
MAKES: 6 SERVINGS

- 6 tsp. butter
- 6 Tbsp. brown sugar
- 6 canned pineapple slices
- 6 maraschino cherries
- 6 individual round sponge cakes

1. Place 1 tsp. butter in 1 side of the sandwich iron. Hold over fire to melt; remove from fire. Carefully sprinkle 1 Tbsp. brown sugar over melted butter. Top with pineapple ring; add cherry to center of pineapple. Top with cake (flat side up); close iron.
2. Cook pineapple side down over a hot campfire until the brown sugar is melted and cake is heated through, 5-8 minutes. Invert iron to open, and serve the cake on an individual plate.
1 cake: 211 cal., 6g fat (3g sat. fat), 38mg chol., 214mg sod., 39g carb. (32g sugars, 1g fiber), 2g pro.

SOURDOUGH BREAD BOWL SANDWICH

SOURDOUGH BREAD BOWL SANDWICH

I created this for when my husband and I go to the lake. I don't like to spend a lot of time hovering over a hot pot or grill, especially in the warm Oklahoma summer months, and this filling sandwich is ready in minutes. For extra flavor, brush melted garlic and herb butter over the top prior to cooking.

—Shawna Welsh-Garrison, Owasso, OK

PREP: 15 MIN. • **COOK:** 25 MIN. + STANDING
MAKES: 8 SERVINGS

- 1 round loaf sourdough bread (1½ lbs.)
- ½ cup honey mustard salad dressing
- 4 slices sharp cheddar cheese
- ⅓ lb. thinly sliced deli ham
- 4 slices smoked provolone cheese
- ⅓ lb. thinly sliced deli smoked turkey
- 1 Tbsp. butter, melted

1. Prepare campfire or grill for low heat. Cut a thin slice from the top of the bread loaf. Hollow out the bottom of the loaf, leaving a ½-in.-thick shell (save removed bread for another use). Spread dressing on inside of hollowed loaf and under the top of the bread. Layer with the cheddar, ham, provolone and turkey. Replace top. Place loaf on a piece of heavy-duty foil (about 24x18 in.). Brush loaf with butter. Fold foil edges over top, crimping to seal.
2. Cook over campfire or grill until loaf is heated through, 25-30 minutes. Let the sandwich stand for 15 minutes before removing foil. Cut into wedges.
1 wedge: 346 cal., 17g fat (6g sat. fat), 46mg chol., 865mg sod., 30g carb. (5g sugars, 1g fiber), 19g pro.

FOURTH OF JULY
FAMILY REUNION

SWEET & TANGY BARBECUED CHICKEN

GREEN BEAN-CHERRY TOMATO SALAD

My grandmother always made a cold green bean salad with potatoes for every family barbecue. Now I bring my own version of the recipes to parties. With added color and taste from the cherry tomatoes, this classic favorite is even better.
—Angela Lemoine, Howell, NJ

PREP: 25 MIN. • **COOK:** 10 MIN.
MAKES: 12 SERVINGS

- 1½ lbs. fresh green beans, trimmed
- 1 pint cherry tomatoes, halved
- 1 small red onion, halved and thinly sliced
- 3 Tbsp. red wine vinegar
- 1½ tsp. sugar
- ¾ tsp. dried oregano
- ¾ tsp. salt
- ¼ tsp. garlic powder
- ¼ tsp. pepper
- ¼ cup olive oil

1. In a 6-qt. stockpot, bring 6 cups water to a boil. Add the beans in batches; cook, uncovered, 2-3 minutes or just until crisp-tender. Remove the beans and immediately drop into ice water. Drain and pat dry.
2. Transfer beans to a large bowl. Add tomatoes and onion; toss to combine. In a small bowl, whisk vinegar, sugar, oregano, salt, garlic powder and pepper. Gradually whisk in oil until blended. Pour over bean mixture; toss to coat.
1 serving: 65 cal., 5g fat (1g sat. fat), 0 chol., 153mg sod., 6g carb. (2g sugars, 2g fiber), 1g pro. **Diabetic exchanges:** 1 vegetable, 1 fat.

SWEET & TANGY BARBECUED CHICKEN

My family loves to grill in the summer, and this has become our hands-down favorite to share with friends. Every bite is full of flavor and the chicken is always tender and juicy.
—Joy Yurk, Grafton, WI

PREP: 15 MIN. + MARINATING • **GRILL:** 30 MIN.
MAKES: 8 SERVINGS

- 2½ cups white wine
- 2 medium onions, finely chopped (1½ cups)
- ½ cup lemon juice
- 10 garlic cloves, minced
- 16 chicken drumsticks
- 3 bay leaves
- 1 can (15 oz.) tomato puree
- ¼ cup honey
- 1 Tbsp. molasses
- 1 tsp. salt
- ½ tsp. dried thyme
- ¼ tsp. cayenne pepper
- ¼ tsp. pepper
- 2 Tbsp. white vinegar

1. For the marinade, in a large bowl, combine wine, onions, lemon juice and garlic. Pour 2 cups of the marinade into a large bowl. Add the chicken and toss to coat. Cover bowl and refrigerate 4 hours or overnight. Add bay leaves to the remaining marinade; cover and refrigerate.
2. Meanwhile, in a large saucepan, combine the tomato puree, honey, molasses, salt, thyme, cayenne, pepper and remaining marinade. Bring to a boil. Reduce the heat; simmer, uncovered, 35-40 minutes or until liquid is reduced by half. Remove from heat. Remove bay leaves; stir in vinegar. Reserve 1 cup sauce for serving; keep warm.
3. Drain the drumsticks, discarding the marinade in the container. Grill chicken, covered, on a greased rack over indirect medium heat 15 minutes. Turn chicken and grill 15-20 minutes longer or until a thermometer reads 170°-175°, brushing occasionally with the remaining sauce. Serve chicken with the reserved sauce.
2 drumsticks with 2 Tbsp. sauce: 334 cal., 12g fat (3g sat. fat), 95mg chol., 398mg sod., 18g carb. (13g sugars, 1g fiber), 30g pro.

HONEY-MELON SALAD WITH BASIL

Put the taste of summer in your salad! With juicy cantaloupe, honeydew and a sweet honey dressing, this dish will be gone in minutes. Watermelon is a great addition, too.
—Khurshid Shaik, Omaha, NE

TAKES: 20 MIN. • **MAKES:** 12 SERVINGS

- 6 cups cubed cantaloupe (about 1 medium)
- 6 cups cubed honeydew melon (about 1 medium)
- ¼ cup honey
- 3 Tbsp. lemon juice
- ½ tsp. paprika
- ¼ tsp. salt
- ¼ tsp. coarsely ground pepper
- ¼ cup minced fresh basil or mint Dried cranberries, optional

In a large bowl, combine cantaloupe and honeydew. Refrigerate, covered, until serving. In a small bowl, whisk honey, lemon juice, paprika, salt and pepper. Pour over melons just before serving; toss to coat. Stir in the basil and, if desired, dried cranberries. Serve with a slotted spoon.
1 cup: 68 cal., 0 fat (0 sat. fat), 0 chol., 72mg sod., 17g carb. (16g sugars, 1g fiber), 1g pro.
Diabetic exchanges: 1 fruit.

PEACH-CHIPOTLE BABY BACK RIBS

PEACH-CHIPOTLE BABY BACK RIBS

My son and I collaborated in the kitchen one day to put our own unique twist on classic baby back ribs. We added a sweet peachy glaze and a little heat with chipotle peppers. It was a great bonding experience, and now we have a keeper recipe for fall-off-the-bone ribs.
—Rebecca Suaso, Weaverville, NC

PREP: 15 MIN. • **BAKE:** 2¾ HOURS
MAKES: 8 SERVINGS (2 CUPS SAUCE)

- 3 Tbsp. brown sugar
- 2 Tbsp. kosher salt
- 1 tsp. pepper
- ½ tsp. cayenne pepper
- 8 lbs. pork baby back ribs (about 3 racks)
- 6 medium peaches, peeled and sliced
- 2 Tbsp. olive oil
- 2 large sweet onions, finely chopped
- ⅔ cup packed brown sugar
- 4 finely chopped chipotle peppers in adobo sauce plus 2 Tbsp. sauce
- 3 Tbsp. white vinegar
- 4 tsp. ground mustard

1. Preheat oven to 325°. In a small bowl, combine brown sugar, salt, pepper and cayenne. If necessary, remove the thin membrane from back ribs; discard the membrane. Rub brown sugar mixture over ribs. Transfer ribs to large roasting pans. Add 1 in. hot water. Bake, covered, until ribs are tender, 2½-3 hours.
2. Meanwhile, place the peaches in a blender; cover and process until smooth. In a large saucepan, heat the oil over medium heat. Add onions; cook and stir until tender, 12-15 minutes. Add brown sugar, chipotle peppers, adobo sauce, vinegar, mustard and peach puree; bring to a boil. Reduce the heat; simmer sauce uncovered, until slightly thickened, 25-30 minutes.
3. Drain the ribs. Grill the ribs, pork side down, covered, on a greased rack over medium heat until meat is browned, 5-7 minutes. Turn the ribs; brush with 2 cups sauce. Cook 5-7 minutes. Serve with remaining sauce.
1 serving with ¼ cup sauce: 788 cal., 48g fat (16g sat. fat), 163mg chol., 1759mg sod., 43g carb. (37g sugars, 3g fiber), 47g pro.

PATRIOTIC
COOKIE & CREAM
CUPCAKES

STRAWBERRY WATERMELON LEMONADE

The nutrition department at my local hospital actually inspired me to create this refreshing summer sipper. I tweaked their recipe to create this drink full of sweet-tart flavor.
—Dawn E. Lowenstein, Huntingdon Valley, PA

TAKES: 20 MIN.
MAKES: 12 SERVINGS

- ¼ cup sugar
- 2 cups boiling water
- ½ lb. fresh strawberries, hulled and quartered (about 2 cups)
- 12 cups cubed watermelon (about 1 medium)
- 1 can (12 oz.) frozen lemonade concentrate, thawed
- 3 Tbsp. lemon juice
  Ice cubes

Dissolve sugar in boiling water. Place strawberries and watermelon in batches in a blender; cover and process until blended. Pour blended fruit though a fine mesh strainer; transfer to a large pitcher. Stir in lemonade concentrate, lemon juice and sugar water. Serve over ice.

1 cup: 119 cal., 0 fat (0 sat. fat), 0 chol., 7mg sod., 34g carb. (30g sugars, 1g fiber), 1g pro.

PATRIOTIC COOKIES & CREAM CUPCAKES

Bring on the red, white and blue with this creative cupcake cake perfect for the Fourth of July, Memorial Day or any festive patriotic occasion. With some delicious and colorful frosting and a careful arrangement, your sweet display will be a nod to the flag.
—Rebecca Wetherbee, Marion, OH

PREP: 40 MIN. • **BAKE:** 20 MIN. + COOLING
MAKES: 2 DOZEN

- ½ cup butter, softened
- 1⅔ cups sugar
- 3 large egg whites, room temperature
- 2 tsp. vanilla extract
- 2¼ cups all-purpose flour
- 3 tsp. baking powder
- ½ tsp. salt
- 1 cup 2% milk
- 1 cup Oreo cookie crumbs

FROSTING
- ¾ cup butter, softened
- 6 cups confectioners' sugar
- ½ tsp. clear or regular vanilla extract
- 3 to 4 Tbsp. 2% milk
  Blue and red paste food coloring
  Star sprinkles

1. Preheat oven to 350°. Line 24 muffin cups with paper or foil liners.

2. In a large bowl, cream butter and sugar until crumbly. Add egg whites, 1 at a time, beating well after each addition. Beat in vanilla. In another bowl, whisk flour, baking powder and salt; add to creamed mixture alternately with milk, beating well after each addition. Fold in cookie crumbs.

3. Fill prepared cups two-thirds full. Bake 20-24 minutes or until a toothpick inserted in center comes out clean. Cool in pans 10 minutes before removing to wire racks to cool completely.

4. In a large bowl, combine butter, confectioners sugar and vanilla; beat until smooth. Add enough milk to make a stiff frosting. Remove 1 cup frosting to a small bowl; tint with blue food coloring. Divide the remaining frosting in half; tint 1 portion red and leave the remaining portion plain.

5. Cut a small hole in the tip of a pastry bag; insert a #1M star pastry tip. Fill the bag with the plain frosting; pipe over 9 cupcakes. With red frosting, pipe 9 more cupcakes. Pipe remaining cupcakes blue; top with star sprinkles. Arrange cupcakes on a large platter, so the colors suggest a flag.

1 cup: 119 cal., 0 fat (0 sat. fat), 0 chol., 7mg sod., 34g carb. (30g sugars, 1g fiber), 1g pro.

SUMMER'S TOP

CONDIMENTS, PRESERVES & MORE

Few things amp up flavor like savory spice blends and tangy sauces. Take ho-hum dishes over the top with mouthwatering—and easy—jams, sauces and canned delights. They'll help you enjoy summer's bounty for months to come.

BASIL & PARSLEY PESTO

⏱ 5i

QUICK & EASY HONEY MUSTARD

This fast, easy mustard, made with rice vinegar and honey, has more flavor than any other honey mustard dressing I've ever tried.
—Sharon Rehm, New Blaine, AR

TAKES: 5 MIN. • **MAKES:** 1 CUP

- ½ cup stone-ground mustard
- ¼ cup honey
- ¼ cup rice vinegar

In a small bowl, whisk all ingredients. Refrigerate until serving.
1 Tbsp.: 28 cal., 1g fat (0 sat. fat), 0 chol., 154mg sod., 6g carb. (5g sugars, 0 fiber), 0 pro.

SAVORY STEAK RUB

Marjoram stars in this recipe. I use the rub on a variety of beef cuts—it locks in the natural juices of the meat for mouthwatering results.
—Donna Brockett, Kingfisher, OK

TAKES: 5 MIN. • **MAKES:** ¼ CUP

- 1 Tbsp. dried marjoram
- 1 Tbsp. dried basil
- 2 tsp. garlic powder
- 2 tsp. dried thyme
- 1 tsp. dried rosemary, crushed
- ¾ tsp. dried oregano

Combine all ingredients; store in an airtight container. Rub over steaks before grilling or broiling. Will season 4-5 steaks.
1 Tbsp.: 12 cal., 0 fat (0 sat. fat), 0 chol., 2mg sod., 3g carb. (0 sugars, 1g fiber), 1g pro.

⏱ ❄

BASIL & PARSLEY PESTO

Toss this herby pesto with pasta, spread it over sandwiches or stir it into an Italian-style soup, such as minestrone.
—Lorraine Stevenski, Land O' Lakes, FL

TAKES: 15 MIN. • **MAKES:** 1¼ CUPS

- 2 cups loosely packed basil leaves
- 1 cup loosely packed Italian parsley
- ¼ cup slivered almonds, toasted
- 2 garlic cloves
- 4 tsp. grated lemon zest
- ⅓ cup lemon juice
- 2 Tbsp. honey
- ½ tsp. salt
- ½ cup olive oil
- ½ cup grated Parmesan cheese

1. Place basil, parsley, almonds and garlic in a small food processor; pulse until chopped. Add lemon zest, juice, honey and salt; process until blended. Continue processing while gradually adding oil in a steady stream. Add cheese; pulse just until blended.
2. Store in an airtight container in the refrigerator for up to 1 week.
Freeze option: Transfer pesto to ice cube trays; cover and freeze pesto until firm. Remove cubes from trays and transfer to a resealable freezer container; return to freezer. To use, thaw cubes in refrigerator 2 hours.
Note: To toast nuts, bake in a shallow pan in a 350° oven for 5-10 minutes or cook in a skillet over low heat until lightly browned, stirring occasionally.
2 Tbsp.: 148 cal., 13g fat (2g sat. fat), 3mg chol., 195mg sod., 6g carb. (4g sugars, 1g fiber), 2g pro.

SPICY
CHUNKY
SALSA

SPICY CHUNKY SALSA

Vinegar adds a refreshing tang to this sweet tomato salsa. It's wonderful as is, but for more heat, leave in some hot pepper seeds.
—Donna Goutermont, Sequim, WA

PREP: 1½ HOURS • **PROCESS:** 15 MIN.
MAKES: 8 PINTS

- 6 lbs. tomatoes
- 3 large green peppers, chopped
- 3 large onions, chopped
- 2 cups white vinegar
- 1 large sweet red pepper, chopped
- 1 can (12 oz.) tomato paste
- 4 jalapeno peppers, seeded and chopped
- 2 serrano peppers, seeded and chopped
- ½ cup sugar
- ½ cup minced fresh cilantro
- ½ cup bottled lemon juice
- 3 garlic cloves, minced
- 4 tsp. ground cumin
- 1 Tbsp. salt
- 2 tsp. dried oregano
- 1 tsp. hot pepper sauce

1. In a Dutch oven, bring 2 qt. water to a boil. Using a slotted spoon, place tomatoes, a few at a time, in boiling water for 30-60 seconds. Remove each tomato and immediately plunge into ice water. Drain and pat dry. Peel and finely chop tomatoes to measure 9 cups; place in a stockpot.

2. Stir in remaining ingredients. Add water to cover; bring to a boil. Reduce heat; simmer, uncovered, until slightly thickened, about 30 minutes.

3. Ladle hot mixture into hot 1-pint jars, leaving ½-in. headspace. Remove any air bubbles and adjust headspace, if necessary, by adding or removing hot mixture. Wipe rims. Center lids on jars; screw on bands until fingertip tight.

4. Place jars into canner with simmering water, ensuring that they are completely covered with the water. Bring to a boil; process for 15 minutes. Carefully remove jars and cool.

Note: Wear disposable gloves when cutting hot peppers; the oils can burn skin. Avoid touching your face.
The processing time listed is for altitudes of 1,000 feet or less. For altitudes up to 3,000 feet, add 5 minutes; 6,000 feet, add 10 minutes; 8,000 feet, add 15 minutes; 10,000 feet, add 20 minutes.

¼ cup: 25 cal., 0 fat (0 sat. fat), 0 chol., 117mg sod., 6g carb. (4g sugars, 1g fiber), 1g pro. **Diabetic exchanges:** ½ starch.

MRS. INA'S CORN RELISH

Mrs. Ina was an older lady who came to our church for many years. She made an amazing corn relish. I whip up my own batch to give to friends at Christmastime.
—Brenda Wooten, Dayton, TN

TAKES: 25 MIN. • **MAKES:** 1½ CUPS

- 1 can (11 oz.) whole kernel corn
- ⅓ cup chopped onion
- ⅓ cup chopped celery
- 3 Tbsp. chopped green pepper
- 3 Tbsp. diced pimientos, drained
- 1 small garlic clove, minced, optional
- ⅓ cup sugar
- 1 tsp. salt
- 1 tsp. celery seed
- 1 tsp. mustard seed
- ¼ tsp. crushed red pepper flakes
- ⅛ tsp. ground ginger
- 1 cup white vinegar, divided
- 1 Tbsp. all-purpose flour
- 1½ tsp. ground mustard
- ¼ tsp. ground turmeric

1. Drain corn, reserving 1 Tbsp. liquid. In a small saucepan, combine the onion, celery, green pepper, pimientos and, if desired, garlic. Stir in sugar, salt, celery seed, mustard seed, pepper flakes, ginger and ¾ cup vinegar. Bring to a boil. Boil 5-7 minutes.

2. In a small bowl, mix flour, mustard and turmeric. Stir in reserved corn liquid until smooth. Add to mixture; stir in the remaining vinegar. Cook, uncovered, 2-3 minutes or until a bit thickened. Add corn; boil 1-2 minutes or until thickened.

¼ cup: 88 cal., 1g fat (0 sat. fat), 0 chol., 550mg sod., 19g carb. (15g sugars, 2g fiber), 2g pro.

GARLIC-PEPPER RUB

This rub adds a tasty mix of garlic, pepper and lemon to any burger. It's a great way to spice up your grilled or broiled foods.
—Ann Marie Moch, Kintyre, ND

TAKES: 5 MIN. • **MAKES:** ⅔ CUP

- 6 Tbsp. lemon-pepper seasoning
- 2 Tbsp. dried thyme
- 2 Tbsp. paprika
- 2 tsp. garlic powder
- 1 tsp. sugar
- ½ tsp. salt
- ¼ tsp. ground coriander
- ⅛ tsp. ground cumin
- ⅛ tsp. cayenne pepper

In a large bowl, combine all ingredients; store in a covered container. Rub over meat or poultry; let stand for at least 30 minutes before grilling or broiling.
1 tsp.: 5 cal., 0 fat (0 sat. fat), 0 chol., 296mg sod., 1g carb. (0 sugars, 0 fiber), 0 pro.

VERY BERRY SPREAD

Two kinds of berries make this spread deliciously different. I always keep some of this jam on hand to enjoy—not only for breakfast, but also as a treat during the day.
—Irene Hagel, Choiceland, SK

PREP: 15 MIN. • **PROCESS:** 10 MIN.
MAKES: ABOUT 8 HALF-PINTS

- 5 cups fresh or frozen raspberries
- 3 cups fresh or frozen blueberries
- 1 Tbsp. bottled lemon juice
- 1 Tbsp. grated lemon zest
- 1 pkg. (1¾ oz.) powdered fruit pectin
- 6 cups sugar

1. In a Dutch oven, combine the berries, lemon juice, zest and pectin. Bring to a full rolling boil over high heat, stirring constantly. Stir in the sugar; return to a full rolling boil. Boil for 1 minute, stirring constantly.
2. Remove from the heat; skim off any foam. Carefully ladle hot mixture into hot half-pint jars, leaving ¼-in. headspace. Remove air bubbles; wipe rims and adjust lids. Process for 10 minutes in a boiling-water canner.
Note: The processing time listed is for altitudes of 1,000 feet or less. Add 1 minute to the processing time for each 1,000 feet of additional altitude.
2 Tbsp.: 86 cal., 0 fat (0 sat. fat), 0 chol., 0 sod., 22g carb. (20g sugars, 1g fiber), 0 pro.

HOMEMADE LEMON CURD

Lemon curd is a scrumptious spread for scones, biscuits or other baked goods. You can find it in larger grocery stores alongside the jams and jellies or with baking supplies, but we like making it from scratch.
—Mark Hagen, Milwaukee, WI

PREP: 20 MIN. + CHILLING • **MAKES:** 1⅔ CUPS

- 3 large eggs
- 1 cup sugar
- ½ cup lemon juice (about 2 lemons)
- ¼ cup butter, cubed
- 1 Tbsp. grated lemon zest

In a small heavy saucepan over medium heat, whisk eggs, sugar and lemon juice until blended. Add butter and lemon zest; cook, whisking constantly, until mixture is thickened and coats the back of a metal spoon. Transfer to a small bowl; cool 10 minutes. Refrigerate, covered, until cold.
2 Tbsp.: 110 cal., 5g fat (3g sat. fat), 52mg chol., 45mg sod., 16g carb. (16g sugars, 0 fiber), 2g pro.

Always use fresh lemon juice for lemon curd, not the bottled variety. The results are much tastier. Don't use pans or spoons of aluminum or unlined copper when making curd. They could react with the acid in the lemons, discoloring the curd and leaving an unpleasant metallic aftertaste.

SWEET & SPICY BARBECUE SAUCE

I've never cared for store-bought barbecue sauce. I like to make things from scratch.
—Helena Georgette Mann, Sacramento, CA

PREP: 30 MIN. • **COOK:** 35 MIN. + COOLING
MAKES: 1½ CUPS

- 1 medium onion, chopped
- 1 Tbsp. canola oil
- 1 garlic clove, minced
- 1 to 3 tsp. chili powder
- ¼ tsp. cayenne pepper
- ¼ tsp. coarsely ground pepper
- 1 cup ketchup
- ⅓ cup molasses
- 2 Tbsp. cider vinegar
- 2 Tbsp. Worcestershire sauce
- 2 Tbsp. spicy brown mustard
- ½ tsp. hot pepper sauce

1. In a large saucepan, saute onion in oil until tender. Add garlic; cook 1 minute. Stir in the chili powder, cayenne and pepper; cook 1 minute longer.
2. Stir in the ketchup, molasses, vinegar, Worcestershire sauce, mustard and pepper sauce. Bring to a boil. Reduce the heat; simmer, uncovered, for 30-40 minutes or until sauce reaches desired consistency. Cool for 15 minutes.
3. Strain the sauce through a fine mesh strainer over a large bowl, discarding vegetables and seasonings. Store in an airtight container in the refrigerator for up to 1 month. Use as a basting sauce for grilled meats.
2 Tbsp.: 68 cal., 1g fat (0 sat. fat), 0 chol., 325mg sod., 14g carb. (11g sugars, 1g fiber), 0 pro.

🟠 CHUNKY PEACH SPREAD

Here's a fruit spread that captures the best tastes of late summer. I like that it's low in sugar and not overly sweet, which lets the fresh peach flavor shine right through.
—Rebecca Baird, Salt Lake City, UT

PREP: 20 MIN. • **COOK:** 10 MIN. + COOLING
MAKES: ABOUT 3½ CUPS

- 7 medium peaches (2 to 2½ lbs.)
- 1 envelope unflavored gelatin
- ¼ cup cold water
- ⅓ cup sugar
- 1 Tbsp. lemon juice

1. Fill a large saucepan two-thirds full with water; bring to a boil. Cut a shallow "X" on the bottom of each peach. Using tongs, place peaches, a few at a time, in boiling water 30-60 seconds or just until skin at the "X" begins to loosen. Remove peaches and immediately drop into ice water. Pull off skins with tip of a knife; discard skins. Chop peaches.
2. In a small bowl, sprinkle gelatin over cold water; let stand 1 minute. In a large saucepan, combine peaches, sugar and lemon juice; bring to a boil. Mash the peaches. Reduce the heat; simmer, uncovered, 5 minutes. Add the gelatin mixture; cook 1 minute longer, stirring until gelatin is completely dissolved. Cool 10 minutes.
3. Pour into jars. Refrigerate, covered, up to 3 weeks.
2 Tbsp.: 25 cal., 0 fat (0 sat. fat), 0 chol., 1mg sod., 6g carb. (5g sugars, 1g fiber), 1g pro.

🟠 STRAWBERRY FREEZER JAM

Our strawberry season is in early June. That's when I use this recipe from a dear friend we met when we lived in Germany. This jam is great on ice cream.
—Mary Jean Ellis, Indianapolis, IN

PREP: 40 MIN. + FREEZING • **MAKES:** 4½ PINTS

- 2 qt. fresh strawberries
- 5½ cups sugar
- 1 cup light corn syrup
- ¼ cup lemon juice
- ¾ cup water
- 1 pkg. (1¾ oz.) powdered fruit pectin

1. Wash and mash berries, measuring out enough mashed berries to make 4 cups; place in a large bowl. Stir in sugar, corn syrup and lemon juice. Let stand 10 minutes.
2. In a Dutch oven, combine the strawberry mixture and water. Stir in pectin. Bring to a full rolling boil over high heat, stirring constantly. Boil 1 minute, stirring constantly. Remove from heat; skim off foam.
3. Pour into jars or freezer containers, leaving ½ in. headspace. Put on lids and let stand overnight or until set, but not longer than 24 hours. Refrigerate up to 3 weeks or freeze up to 12 months.
2 Tbsp.: 79 cal., 0 fat (0 sat. fat), 0 chol., 3mg sod., 20g carb. (20g sugars, 0 fiber), 0 pro.

BEST EVER
SWEET PICKLE

BEST EVER SWEET PICKLES

When I was a kid, I always looked forward to the homemade jams and jellies my granny made from her farm-grown berries. Our urban backyard doesn't have room for a berry patch, but we do have a trellis for growing cucumbers. I pack away these sweet pickles every summer.
—Ellie Martin Cliffe, Milwaukee, WI

PREP: 1 HOUR + STANDING
PROCESS: 10 MIN. • **MAKES:** 4 PINTS

- 9 cups sliced pickling cucumbers
- 1 large sweet onion, halved and thinly sliced
- ¼ cup canning salt
- 1 cup sugar
- 1 cup water
- 1 cup white vinegar
- ½ cup cider vinegar
- 2 Tbsp. mustard seed
- 1 tsp. celery seed
- ½ tsp. whole peppercorns
- 4 bay leaves
- 12 garlic cloves, crushed

1. In a large nonreactive bowl, combine cucumbers, onion and salt. Cover with crushed ice; mix well. Let stand 3 hours. Drain; rinse and drain thoroughly.
2. In a Dutch oven, combine the sugar, water, vinegars, mustard seed, celery seed and peppercorns. Bring to a boil, stirring to dissolve the sugar. Add the cucumber mixture; return to a boil, stirring occasionally. Reduce the heat; simmer, uncovered, 4-5 minutes or until heated through.
3. Carefully ladle hot mixture into 4 hot wide-mouth 1-pint jars, leaving ½-in. headspace. Add 3 garlic cloves and 1 bay leaf to each jar. Remove air bubbles and, if necessary, adjust headspace by adding hot pickling liquid. Wipe rims. Center the lids on jars; screw on the bands until fingertip tight.
4. Carefully place jars into canner with simmering water, ensuring that they are completely covered with the water. Bring to a boil; process for 10 minutes. Remove jars and cool.
¼ cup: 35 cal., 0 fat (0 sat. fat), 0 chol., 175mg sod., 8g carb. (7g sugars, 0 fiber), 0 pro.

HOMEMADE CANNED SPAGHETTI SAUCE

HOMEMADE CANNED SPAGHETTI SAUCE

This spaghetti sauce is a tomato grower's dream come true! You can use up your garden bounty and enjoy it later in the year.
—Tonya Branham, Mount Olive, AL

PREP: 1½ HOURS + SIMMERING
PROCESS: 40 MIN. • **MAKES:** 9 QT.

- 25 lbs. tomatoes (about 80 medium)
- 4 large green peppers, seeded
- 4 large onions, cut into wedges
- 2 cans (12 oz. each) tomato paste
- ¼ cup canola oil
- ⅔ cup sugar
- ¼ cup salt
- 8 garlic cloves, minced
- 4 tsp. dried oregano
- 2 tsp. dried parsley flakes
- 2 tsp. dried basil
- 2 tsp. crushed red pepper flakes
- 2 tsp. Worcestershire sauce
- 2 bay leaves
- 1 cup plus 2 Tbsp. bottled lemon juice

1. In a Dutch oven, bring 2 qt. water to a boil. Using a slotted spoon, place the tomatoes, 1 at a time, in boiling water for 30-60 seconds. Remove each tomato and immediately plunge into ice water.

Peel and quarter tomatoes; place in a stockpot.
2. Pulse green peppers and onions in batches in a food processor until finely chopped; transfer to stockpot. Stir in next 11 ingredients. Add water to cover; bring to a boil. Reduce heat and simmer, uncovered, 4-5 hours; stir occasionally.
3. Discard bay leaves. Add 2 Tbsp. lemon juice to each of 9 hot 1-qt. jars. Carefully ladle hot mixture into jars, leaving ½-in. headspace. Remove the air bubbles and adjust the headspace, if necessary, by adding or removing hot mixture. Wipe rims. Center lids on jars; screw on bands until fingertip tight.
4. Place jars into canner with simmering water, ensuring that they are completely covered with water. Bring to a boil and process for 40 minutes. Remove jars and cool.
Note: The processing time listed is for altitudes of 1,000 feet or less. For altitudes up to 3,000 feet, add 5 minutes; 6,000 feet, add 10 minutes; 8,000 feet, add 15 minutes; 10,000 feet, add 20 minutes.
¾ cup: 118 cal., 5g fat (0 sat. fat), 0 chol., 614mg sod., 17g carb. (11g sugars, 4g fiber), 3g pro. **Diabetic exchanges:** 1 starch, 1 fat.

SUMMER'S COOLEST

FROSTY TREATS

Top off those lazy, hazy days of summer with icy treats from the freezer. From casual to impressive, these frosty favorites tempt everyone's sweet tooth. Homemade ice cream, hand-held pops, colorful sundaes and frozen cakes make any day brighter.

THOMAS JEFFERSON'S VANILLA ICE CREAM

WATERMELON CHOCOLATE CHIP SORBET

Summertime and watermelon go hand in hand. My melon sorbet is fresh, fruity and without the gluten and eggs you get in many other frozen desserts.
—Rachel Lewis, Danville, VA

PREP: 15 MIN. + CHILLING
PROCESS: 30 MIN. + FREEZING
MAKES: 1 QT.

- 1 cup sugar
- ½ cup water
- 3 cups chopped seedless watermelon
- 1 cup orange juice
- 2 Tbsp. lime juice
- ½ cup miniature semisweet chocolate chips, optional

1. In a small saucepan, bring sugar and water to a boil. Reduce heat; simmer, uncovered, 5 minutes, stirring liquid occasionally to dissolve the sugar. Cool slightly.
2. Place watermelon in a food processor; process until pureed. Add orange juice, lime juice and cooled syrup; process until blended. Transfer to a large bowl; refrigerate, covered, until cold, about 3 hours.
3. Pour into cylinder of ice cream freezer. Freeze according to the manufacturer's directions; if desired, add chocolate chips during the last 10 minutes of processing. Transfer sorbet to freezer containers, allowing headspace for expansion. Freeze until firm, 2-4 hours.
½ cup: 129 cal., 0 fat (0 sat. fat), 0 chol., 1mg sod., 33g carb. (32g sugars, 0 fiber), 1g pro.

THOMAS JEFFERSON'S VANILLA ICE CREAM

The third U.S. president is credited with jotting down the first American recipe for this treat. Don't have vanilla bean on hand? Substitute a tablespoon vanilla extract for the vanilla bean. Just stir the extract into the cream mixture after the ice-water bath.
—*Taste of Home* Test Kitchen

PREP: 15 MIN. + CHILLING
PROCESS: 20 MIN./BATCH + FREEZING
MAKES: 2¼ QT.

- 2 qt. heavy whipping cream
- 1 cup sugar
- 1 vanilla bean
- 6 large egg yolks

1. In a large heavy saucepan, combine cream and sugar. Split vanilla bean in half lengthwise. With a sharp knife, scrape seeds into pan; add bean. Heat cream mixture over medium heat until bubbles form around side of pan, stirring to dissolve sugar.
2. In a small bowl, whisk a little of the hot mixture into the egg yolks; return all to the pan, whisking constantly.
3. Cook over low heat until mixture is just thick enough to coat a metal spoon and the temperature reaches 160°, stirring constantly. Do not allow mixture to boil. Immediately transfer to a bowl.
4. Place bowl in a pan of ice water. Stir gently and occasionally for 2 minutes; discard vanilla bean. Press waxed paper onto surface of the custard. Refrigerate several hours or overnight.
5. Fill cylinder of ice cream freezer two-thirds full; freeze according to the manufacturer's directions. (Refrigerate remaining mixture until ready to freeze.) Transfer the ice cream to a freezer container; freeze for 4-6 hours or until firm. Repeat with remaining mixture.
½ cup: 424 cal., 40g fat (25g sat. fat), 182mg chol., 32mg sod., 14g carb. (14g sugars, 0 fiber), 4g pro.

FRIED ICE CREAM DESSERT BARS

❄ FRIED ICE CREAM DESSERT BARS

Fried ice cream is such a delicious treat, but it can be a hassle to make the individual servings. This recipe gives you the same fabulous flavor in an easy and convenient bar form.
—Andrea Price, Grafton, WI

PREP: 25 MIN. + FREEZING
COOK: 5 MIN. + COOLING
MAKES: 16 SERVINGS

- ½ cup butter, cubed
- 2 cups crushed cornflakes
- 1½ tsp. ground cinnamon
- 3 Tbsp. sugar
- 1¾ cups heavy whipping cream
- ¼ cup evaporated milk
- ⅛ tsp. salt
- 1 can (14 oz.) sweetened condensed milk
- 2 tsp. vanilla extract
  Optional: Honey, whipped cream and maraschino cherries

1. In a large skillet, melt butter over medium heat. Add the cornflakes and cinnamon; cook and stir until golden brown, about 5 minutes. Remove from heat; stir in the sugar. Cool completely.
2. In a large bowl, beat the cream, evaporated milk and salt until mixture begins to thicken. Gradually beat in the condensed milk and vanilla until mixture is thickened.
3. Sprinkle half of the cornflakes onto bottom of a greased 9-in. square baking pan. Pour the filling over the crust and sprinkle with the remaining cornflakes. Cover and freeze overnight. Cut into bars. If desired, serve with honey, whipped cream and cherries.
1 bar: 276 cal., 18g fat (11g sat. fat), 55mg chol., 187mg sod., 27g carb. (18g sugars, 0 fiber), 4g pro.

5ⁱ CHOCOLATE FRAMBOISE PARFAITS

Having unexpected company? Make a fabulous dessert in minutes and relieve some of the stress of presenting a beautiful finish to the meal! It doesn't get any easier than these quick, delicious parfaits.
—Charlene Chambers, Ormond Beach, FL

PREP: 15 MIN. + FREEZING
MAKES: 6 SERVINGS

- 6 Tbsp. raspberry liqueur
- 1½ pints vanilla ice cream
- 1½ pints fresh raspberries
- 2¼ cups chocolate wafer crumbs
  Sweetened whipped cream

Layer each of 6 parfait glasses with 1 tsp. raspberry liqueur, 2½ Tbsp. ice cream, 4 or 5 raspberries and 2 Tbsp. chocolate wafer crumbs. Repeat the layers twice. Freeze. To serve, top with the whipped cream and the remaining raspberries.
1 parfait: 402 cal., 14g fat (6g sat. fat), 30mg chol., 297mg sod., 59g carb. (38g sugars, 6g fiber), 6g pro.

**CREAMY LAYERED
BLUEBERRY ICE POPS**

❄ CREAMY LAYERED BLUEBERRY ICE POPS

These delicious ice pops can be made with raspberries or blackberries. The rosemary sprig and lemon rind brings another layer of flavor. They're quick and easy, kid-friendly, make-ahead and freezable.

—Gloria Bradley, Naperville, IL

PREP: 25 MIN. + FREEZING
COOK: 10 MIN. + COOLING
MAKES: 10 SERVINGS

- ⅓ cup agave nectar
- ¼ cup water
- 1 fresh rosemary sprig
- 1 lemon zest strip (2 in.)
- 1 Tbsp. lemon juice
- 2 cups fresh or frozen blueberries
- 2 Tbsp. sugar
- 2¼ cups frozen whipped topping, thawed
- 10 freezer pop molds or 10 paper cups (3 oz. each) and wooden pop sticks

1. Place the first 4 ingredients in a small saucepan; bring to a boil, stirring occasionally. Remove from the heat; let stand, covered, 10 minutes. Remove the rosemary and lemon zest. Stir in lemon juice; cool completely.
2. Place the blueberries and sugar in another saucepan; cook and stir over medium heat until the berries pop, about 5-7 minutes. Cool completely.
3. Add whipped topping to the lemon syrup, whisking to blend. Transfer half of the mixture to pastry bag. Pipe into molds. Layer with blueberries. Pipe the remaining whipped topping mixture over top. Close molds with holders. For paper cups, top with foil and insert the sticks through foil.
4. Freeze until firm, about 4 hours. To serve, dip pop molds briefly in warm water before removing.
1 pop: 104 cal., 3g fat (3g sat. fat), 0 chol., 0 sod., 19g carb. (18g sugars, 1g fiber), 0 pro. **Diabetic exchanges:** 1 starch, ½ fat.

Lime flavor would be great in this recipe. Substitute equal parts of lime zest and juice for lemon zest and juice.

WARM PINEAPPLE SUNDAES WITH RUM SAUCE

WARM PINEAPPLE SUNDAES WITH RUM SAUCE

Pineapple, rum and sugar are already a flavorful dream together, but adding ginger and butter really takes this dessert to another level.

—Jamie Miller, Maple Grove, MN

TAKES: 25 MIN. • **MAKES:** 2 SERVINGS

- 4 fresh pineapple spears (about 8 oz.)
- ½ cup packed brown sugar
- 2 Tbsp. dark rum
- ¾ tsp. ground ginger
- 4 tsp. butter, cut into small pieces
- 2 scoops vanilla ice cream or low-fat frozen yogurt
- 4 gingersnap cookies, crushed

1. Place pineapple in 1-qt. baking dish. In a small bowl, combine the brown sugar, rum and ginger; spoon over pineapple. Dot with butter.
2. Bake, uncovered, at 425° until the pineapple is lightly browned and sauce is bubbly, 8-10 minutes. Place ice cream in 2 dessert dishes; top with pineapple and sauce. Serve immediately with the crushed cookies.
1 serving: 536 cal., 16g fat (10g sat. fat), 49mg chol., 221mg sod., 95g carb. (78g sugars, 2g fiber), 4g pro.

HERE'S THE SCOOP

What's in a name? A lot, when it comes to frosty treats. Here's a rundown of the most popular frozen sweets.

ICE CREAM

This all-time popular dessert contains about 10% butterfat, but some premium brands use a slightly higher percentage for a creamier product.

SHERBET

Made from fruit juice, a milk product, sugar and water, this treat has a lighter texture than ice cream and is often sweeter. Some versions might contain fruit, spices or even chocolate.

SORBET

This freezer sweet is made from pureed fruit, sugar and water. It doesn't contain milk or other diary products. Some are flavored with liqueur or wine.

❄ BLACKBERRY DAIQUIRI SHERBET

When I decided to try making sherbet, which is one of my favorites, blackberries were in season in my mom's garden. I love the flavor of daiquiris, and the lime and rum blend with the juicy blackberries beautifully!
—Shelly Bevington, Hermiston, OR

PREP: 15 MIN. • **PROCESS:** 30 MIN. + FREEZING
MAKES: 1¼ QT.

- 3 cups fresh or frozen blackberries, thawed
- 1 cup sugar
- ¼ tsp. salt
- 1 can (12 oz.) evaporated milk
- 2 Tbsp. lime juice
- 1 tsp. rum extract
- ½ tsp. citric acid

1. Place blackberries, sugar and salt in a food processor; process until smooth. Press through a fine-mesh strainer into a bowl; discard seeds and pulp. Stir the remaining ingredients into puree.
2. Fill the cylinder of ice cream maker no more than two-thirds full; freeze according to manufacturer's directions. Transfer sherbet to freezer containers, allowing headspace for expansion. Freeze until firm, 8 hours or overnight.
½ cup: 147 cal., 3g fat (2g sat. fat), 12mg chol., 96mg sod., 28g carb. (26g sugars, 2g fiber), 3g pro.

Substituting rum for the extract might seem like a fun idea but the alcohol will actually keep your daiquiri dessert from freezing solid.

❄ FROZEN KEY LIME DELIGHT

In the middle of summer, nothing hits the spot quite like this sublime Key lime dessert.
—Melissa Millwood, Lyman, SC

PREP: 50 MIN. • **BAKE:** 25 MIN. + FREEZING
MAKES: 8 SERVINGS

- 1 cup all-purpose flour
- ½ cup salted cashews, chopped
- ½ cup sweetened shredded coconut
- ¼ cup packed light brown sugar
- ½ cup butter, melted
- 2 cups heavy whipping cream
- 1½ cups sweetened condensed milk
- 1 cup Key lime juice
- 3 tsp. grated Key lime zest
- 1 tsp. vanilla extract
  Optional: Whipped cream and Key lime slices

1. Preheat oven to 350°. In a small bowl, combine the flour, cashews, coconut and brown sugar. Stir in butter. Sprinkle into a greased 15x10x1-in. baking pan. Bake 20-25 minutes or until golden brown, stirring once. Cool on a wire rack.
2. Meanwhile, in a large bowl, combine cream, milk, lime juice, zest and vanilla. Refrigerate until chilled.
3. Fill cylinder of an ice cream freezer two-thirds full; freeze according to the manufacturer's directions.
4. Sprinkle half of the cashew mixture into an ungreased 11x7-in. dish. Spread the ice cream over top; sprinkle with the remaining cashew mixture. Cover and freeze for 4 hours or until firm. Garnish servings with whipped cream and lime slices if desired.
1 piece: 672 cal., 46g fat (27g sat. fat), 131mg chol., 258mg sod., 60g carb. (42g sugars, 1g fiber), 9g pro.

❄ BANANA SPLIT ICEBOX CAKE

One day a friend showed me how to make a traditional icebox cake with just cream and graham crackers. I make it extra special with the fruit. Now everyone at your potluck can have a banana split without fuss!
—Shelly Flye, Albion, ME

PREP: 30 MIN. + CHILLING
MAKES: 10 SERVINGS

- 1 carton (16 oz.) frozen whipped topping, thawed
- 1 cup sour cream
- 1 pkg. (3.4 oz.) instant vanilla pudding mix
- 1 can (8 oz.) crushed pineapple, drained
- 24 whole graham crackers
- 2 medium bananas, sliced
  Toppings: Chocolate syrup, halved fresh strawberries and additional banana slices

1. In a large bowl, mix the whipped topping, sour cream and pudding mix until blended; fold in pineapple. Cut a small hole in the tip of a pastry bag. Transfer pudding mixture to bag.
2. On a flat serving plate, arrange 4 crackers in a rectangle. Pipe about 1 cup pudding mixture over crackers; top with about ¼ cup banana slices. Repeat layers 5 times. Refrigerate, covered, overnight.
3. Just before serving, top with chocolate syrup, strawberries and additional banana slices.
1 piece: 405 cal., 15g fat (11g sat. fat), 16mg chol., 372mg sod., 60g carb. (30g sugars, 2g fiber), 4g pro.

❋ PATRIOTIC ICE CREAM CUPCAKES

These cupcakes feature red velvet cake, blue moon ice cream, a creamy white topping and star-spangled sprinkles.
—*Taste of Home* Test Kitchen

PREP: 30 MIN. + FREEZING
BAKE: 15 MIN. + COOLING • **MAKES:** 3 DOZEN

- 1 pkg. red velvet cake mix (regular size)
- 1½ qt. blue moon ice cream, softened if necessary
- 1 jar (7 oz.) marshmallow creme
- 3 cups heavy whipping cream
  Red, white and blue sprinkles

1. Preheat oven to 350°. Line 36 muffin cups with paper liners.
2. Prepare cake batter according to package directions. Fill prepared cups about one-third full. Bake until toothpick inserted in the center comes out clean, 11-14 minutes. Cool 10 minutes before removing from pans to wire racks; cool cupcakes completely.
3. Working quickly, spread ice cream onto the cupcakes. Freeze until firm, at least 1 hour.
4. Place marshmallow creme in a large bowl. Add whipping cream; beat until blended and stiff peaks form. Pipe or spread over cupcakes. Decorate with sprinkles. Serve immediately or freeze until firm.
Note: Blue moon ice cream may be substituted with vanilla ice cream tinted with blue food coloring.
1 cupcake: 220 cal., 13g fat (6g sat. fat), 46mg chol., 139mg sod., 21g carb. (16g sugars, 0 fiber), 4g pro.

🔟 ❋ ROCKY ROAD FUDGE POPS

These sweet frozen treats are simple to prepare and guaranteed to bring out the kid in anyone. The creamy pops feature a special chocolate chip and peanut topping.
—Karen Grant, Tulare, CA

PREP: 20 MIN. + FREEZING
MAKES: 12 SERVINGS

- 2½ cups 2% milk
- 1 pkg. (3.4 oz.) cook-and-serve chocolate pudding mix
- ½ cup chopped peanuts
- ½ cup miniature semisweet chocolate chips
- 12 paper cups (3 oz. each)
- ½ cup marshmallow creme
- 12 wooden pop sticks

1. In a large microwave-safe bowl, whisk milk and pudding mix. Microwave, uncovered, on high for 4-6 minutes or until the mixture is bubbly and slightly thickened, stirring every 2 minutes. Cool for 20 minutes, stirring several times.
2. Meanwhile, combine peanuts and chocolate chips; divide among cups. Stir the marshmallow creme into pudding; spoon into cups. Insert wooden pop sticks; freeze.
1 pop: 140 cal., 7g fat (3g sat. fat), 7mg chol., 64mg sod., 18g carb. (14g sugars, 1g fiber), 4g pro.

🔟 ❋ RASPBERRY-BANANA SOFT SERVE

When I make this ice cream, I mix and match bananas for their ripeness. Very ripe ones add more banana flavor. Less ripe ones have a fluffier texture.
—Melissa Hansen, Ellison Bay, WI

PREP: 10 MIN. + FREEZING • **MAKES:** 2½ CUPS

- 4 medium ripe bananas
- ½ cup fat-free plain yogurt
- 1 to 2 Tbsp. maple syrup
- ½ cup frozen unsweetened raspberries
  Fresh raspberries, optional

1. Thinly slice bananas; transfer to a large resealable freezer container. Arrange slices in a single layer; freeze fruit overnight.
2. Pulse bananas in a food processor until finely chopped. Add the yogurt, maple syrup and raspberries. Process just until smooth, scraping the inside of the bowl as needed. Serve immediately, adding fresh berries if desired.
½ cup: 104 cal., 0 fat (0 sat. fat), 1mg chol., 15mg sod., 26g carb. (15g sugars, 2g fiber), 2g pro. **Diabetic exchanges:** 1 fruit, ½ starch.

SUMMER'S MOST

DECADENT DESSERTS

Brilliant berries, juicy fruits, toasted marshmallows, cool and creamy bites, and tangy citrus delights—these are the hallmarks of summer desserts. Cap off backyard barbecues and busy weeknights alike by serving any of these lip-smacking dinner finales.

GRAFFITI CUTOUT COOKIES

Talk about playing with your food! An edible color spray lets you create ombre and color blends unlike other decorating techniques. To create the ombre effect, hold a sheet of paper over already-painted sections as you add layers the color.

—Shannon Norris, Cudahy, WI

PREP: 30 MIN.+ FREEZING
BAKE: 15 MIN. + COOLING
MAKES: 15 COOKIES

¼ cup butter, softened
½ cup sugar
1 large egg, room temperature
1 tsp. vanilla extract
2 cups almond flour
¼ tsp. salt
¼ tsp. baking soda
ROYAL ICING
2 cups confectioners' sugar
2 to 6 Tbsp. water
5 tsp. meringue powder
 Food color spray

1. In a bowl, cream butter and sugar until light and fluffy, 5-7 minutes. Beat in egg and vanilla. In another bowl, whisk the almond flour, salt and baking soda; gradually beat into creamed mixture.
2. Preheat oven to 325°. Between 2 pieces of waxed paper, roll dough to ¼-in. thickness. Place on a cutting board in the freezer until firm, about 20 minutes. Remove paper; cut with 3-in. cookie cutters. Place 2 in. apart on parchment-lined baking sheets.
3. Bake until lightly browned on the edges, 12-15 minutes. Cool on pans 2 minutes. Remove to wire racks to cool completely. For icing, in a large bowl, combine confectioners' sugar, 2 Tbsp. water and meringue powder; beat on low speed just until blended. Beat on high 4-5 minutes or until stiff peaks form. Add additional water as necessary to reach desired consistency. Keep unused icing covered at all times with a damp cloth. If necessary, beat again on high speed to restore texture.
4. Frost cookies and let stand at room temperature several hours or until frosting is dry and firm. Decorate as desired with color spray mist. Store in an airtight container.
1 cookie: 209 cal., 11g fat (3g sat. fat), 21mg chol., 103mg sod., 26g carb. (23g sugars, 2g fiber), 4g pro.

S'MORES CREME BRULEE

S'MORES CREME BRULEE

A big bite into a scrumptious s'more brings back sweet campfire memories. This fancy take on the classic treat is perfect for a fall meal and will be adored by children and adults alike.

—Rose Denning, Overland Park, KS

PREP: 30 MIN. • **BAKE:** 25 MIN. + CHILLING
MAKES: 6 SERVINGS

1 cup 2% milk
3 large eggs, room temperature
⅔ cup sugar
⅓ cup baking cocoa
2 Tbsp. coffee liqueur or strong brewed coffee
⅔ cup graham cracker crumbs
2 Tbsp. butter, melted
⅓ cup sugar or coarse sugar
2 cups miniature marshmallows
1 milk chocolate candy bar (1.55 oz.), broken into 12 pieces

1. Preheat oven to 325°. In a small saucepan, heat the milk until bubbles form around sides of pan; remove from heat. In a large bowl, whisk eggs, sugar, cocoa and liqueur until blended but not foamy. Slowly whisk in hot milk.
2. Place six 4-oz. broiler-safe ramekins in a baking pan large enough to hold them without touching. Pour egg mixture into ramekins. Place pan on oven rack; add very hot water to pan to within ½ in. of top of ramekins. Bake 20-25 minutes or until a knife inserted in the center comes out clean; centers will still be soft. Remove ramekins from water bath immediately to a wire rack; cool 10 minutes. Refrigerate until cold.
3. In a small bowl, mix cracker crumbs and butter; set aside. To caramelize topping with a kitchen torch, sprinkle custards evenly with sugar. Hold torch flame about 2 in. above custard surface and rotate it slowly until sugar is evenly caramelized. Sprinkle the custards with crumb mixture; top with marshmallows. Using torch, heat marshmallows until browned. Top with the chocolate pieces. Serve immediately or refrigerate up to 1 hour.
Note: To caramelize topping in a broiler, place ramekins on a baking sheet; let stand at room temperature 15 minutes. Preheat broiler. Sprinkle the custards evenly with sugar. Broil 3-4 in. from heat 3-5 minutes or until the sugar is caramelized. Sprinkle custards with crumb mixture; top with marshmallows. Broil for 30-45 seconds or until the marshmallows are browned. Top with chocolate pieces. Serve immediately or refrigerate up to 1 hour.
1 serving: 419 cal., 11g fat (5g sat. fat), 108mg chol., 163mg sod., 74g carb. (59g sugars, 2g fiber), 7g pro.

SKILLET BLUEBERRY SLUMP

My mother-in-law made a slump of wild blueberries with dumplings and served it warm with a pitcher of farm cream. We've been eating slump for nearly 60 years!
—Eleanore Ebeling, Brewster, MN

PREP: 25 MIN. • **BAKE:** 20 MIN.
MAKES: 6 SERVINGS

- 4 cups fresh or frozen blueberries
- ½ cup sugar
- ½ cup water
- 1 tsp. grated lemon zest
- 1 Tbsp. lemon juice
- 1 cup all-purpose flour
- 2 Tbsp. sugar
- 2 tsp. baking powder
- ½ tsp. salt
- 1 Tbsp. butter
- ½ cup 2% milk
  Vanilla ice cream

1. Preheat oven to 400°. In a 10-in. ovenproof skillet, combine the first 5 ingredients; bring to a boil. Reduce heat; simmer, uncovered, 9-11 minutes or until mixture is slightly thickened, stirring occasionally.
2. Meanwhile, in a small bowl, whisk the flour, sugar, baking powder and salt. Cut in the butter until mixture resembles coarse crumbs. Add the milk; stir just until moistened.
3. Drop batter in 6 portions on top of the simmering blueberry mixture. Transfer to oven. Bake, uncovered, 17-20 minutes or until the dumplings are golden brown. Serve warm with ice cream.
1 serving: 239 cal., 3g fat (2g sat. fat), 7mg chol., 355mg sod., 52g carb. (32g sugars, 3g fiber), 4g pro.

TART & TANGY LEMON TART

TART & TANGY LEMON TART

Our family adores lemon desserts. I like to make this citrus tart for brunch. For extra special events, I bake it in my heart-shaped tart pan.
—Joyce Moynihan, Lakeville, MN

PREP: 15 MIN. + CHILLING
BAKE: 45 MIN. + COOLING
MAKES: 14 SERVINGS

- ¾ cup butter, softened
- ½ cup confectioners' sugar
- 1½ cups all-purpose flour
FILLING
- ¾ cup sugar
- 1 Tbsp. grated lemon zest
- ¾ cup lemon juice
- 3 large eggs, room temperature
- 3 large egg yolks, room temperature
- 4 oz. cream cheese, softened
- 1 Tbsp. cornstarch
  Sweetened whipped cream, optional

1. Preheat oven to 325°. In a large bowl, cream the butter and confectioners' sugar until smooth. Gradually beat in flour. Press dough onto bottom and up side of an ungreased 11-in. fluted tart pan with removable bottom. Refrigerate 15 minutes.
2. Line unpricked crust with a double thickness of foil. Fill with pie weights, dried beans or uncooked rice. Bake until the crust edge is lightly browned, 18-22 minutes. Remove foil and weights; bake until the bottom is golden brown, 5-7 minutes longer. Cool on a wire rack.
3. In a large bowl, beat the sugar, lemon zest, lemon juice, eggs, egg yolks, cream cheese and cornstarch until blended; pour into crust. Bake until filling is set, 18-22 minutes. Cool on a wire rack. If desired, serve with whipped cream. Refrigerate leftovers.
Note: Let pie weights cool before storing. Beans and rice may be reused for pie weights, but not for cooking.
1 piece: 254 cal., 15g fat (9g sat. fat), 114mg chol., 125mg sod., 27g carb. (16g sugars, 0 fiber), 4g pro.

BERRY-PATCH BROWNIE PIZZA

STRAWBERRY LEMON CUPCAKES

My granddaughter Sydney has developed a love of baking. While I was visiting her in Tampa, we made these light, fluffy cupcakes. She's a natural—these turned out fantastic!
—Lonnie Hartstack, Clarinda, IA

PREP: 15 MIN. • **BAKE:** 20 MIN. + COOLING
MAKES: 2 DOZEN

- 1 **pkg. white cake mix (regular size)**
- 3 **large eggs, room temperature**
- ½ **cup 2% milk**
- ⅓ **cup canola oil**
- 2 **Tbsp. grated lemon zest**
- 3 **Tbsp. lemon juice**
FROSTING
- 4 **cups confectioners' sugar**
- 1 **cup butter, softened**
- ¼ **cup crushed fresh strawberries**

1. Preheat oven to 350°. Line 24 muffin cups with paper liners.
2. In a large bowl, combine the first 6 ingredients; beat on low 30 seconds. Beat on medium 2 minutes. Fill the prepared cups half full. Bake until a toothpick inserted in the center comes out clean, 18-20 minutes. Cool in pans 10 minutes before removing to wire racks to cool completely.
3. For frosting, in a large bowl, combine all ingredients; beat until smooth. Frost the cupcakes. Garnish with additional strawberries. Store in the refrigerator.
1 cupcake: 253 cal., 12g fat (6g sat. fat), 44mg chol., 198mg sod., 35g carb. (27g sugars, 1g fiber), 2g pro.

BERRY-PATCH BROWNIE PIZZA

I just love the combination of fruit, almonds and chocolate that makes this brownie so distinctive. The fruit lightens the chocolate a bit and makes it feel as though you're eating something both decadent and healthy.
—Sue Kauffman, Columbia City, IN

PREP: 20 MIN. + CHILLING
BAKE: 15 MIN. + COOLING
MAKES: 12 SERVINGS

- 1 **pkg. fudge brownie mix (13x9-in. pan size)**
- ⅓ **cup chopped unblanched almonds**
- 1 **tsp. almond extract**
TOPPING
- 1 **pkg. (8 oz.) cream cheese, softened**
- 1 **Tbsp. sugar**
- 1 **tsp. vanilla extract**
- ½ **tsp. grated lemon zest**
- 2 **cups whipped topping**
  Assorted fresh berries
  Optional: Fresh mint leaves and coarse sugar

1. Preheat oven to 375°. Prepare brownie batter according to package directions for fudgelike brownies, adding chopped almonds and almond extract. Spread into a greased 14-in. pizza pan.
2. Bake until a toothpick inserted in the center comes out clean, 15-18 minutes. Cool completely on a wire rack.
3. Beat first 4 topping ingredients until smooth; fold in whipped topping. Spread over the crust to within ½ in. of the edge; refrigerate, loosely covered, 2 hours.
4. To serve, cut the pizza into slices; top with berries of choice. If desired, top with mint and sprinkle with coarse sugar.
1 piece: 404 cal., 26g fat (8g sat. fat), 51mg chol., 240mg sod., 39g carb. (26g sugars, 2g fiber), 5g pro.

BLUE-RIBBON APPLE PIE

With its hidden layer of walnuts, this pie is special to me because I won a blue ribbon for it at the local fair.

—Collette Gaugler, Fogelsville, PA

PREP: 45 MIN.
BAKE: 55 MINUTES + COOLING
MAKES: 8 SERVINGS

CRUST
  Dough for double-crust pie
WALNUT LAYER
  ¾ cup ground walnuts
  2 Tbsp. brown sugar
  2 Tbsp. lightly beaten egg
  1 Tbsp. butter, melted
  1 Tbsp. 2% milk
  ¼ tsp. lemon juice
  ¼ tsp. vanilla extract
FILLING
  6 cups sliced peeled tart apples
    (4-5 medium)
  2 tsp. lemon juice
  ½ tsp. vanilla extract
  ¾ cup sugar
  3 Tbsp. all-purpose flour
  1¼ tsp. ground cinnamon
  ¼ tsp. ground nutmeg
  ⅛ tsp. salt
  3 Tbsp. butter, cubed
TOPPING
  1 tsp. 2% milk
  2 tsp. sugar

1. Preheat oven to 375°. On a lightly floured surface, roll 1 half of dough to a ⅛-in.-thick circle; transfer to a 9-in. pie plate. Trim dough even with the rim.
2. In a small bowl, mix walnut layer ingredients until blended. Spread onto bottom of crust. Refrigerate while preparing the filling.
3. For filling, in a large bowl, toss apples with lemon juice and vanilla. In a small bowl, mix sugar, flour, cinnamon, nutmeg and salt; add to the apple mixture and toss to coat.
4. Pour the filling over walnut layer; dot with butter. Roll remaining dough to a ⅛-in.-thick circle. Place over filling. Trim, seal and flute edge. Brush top with milk; sprinkle with sugar. Cut slits in dough.
5. Place the pie on a baking sheet. Bake 55-65 minutes or until crust is golden brown and filling is bubbly. Cover the edge loosely with foil during the last 10 minutes if needed to prevent any overbrowning. Remove foil. Cool on a wire rack.

Dough for double-crust pie (9 in.): Combine 2½ cups all-purpose flour and ½ tsp. salt; cut in 1 cup shortening until crumbly. Gradually add 4-5 Tbsp. ice water, tossing with a fork until the dough holds together when pressed. Divide the dough in half and shape into disks; wrap and refrigerate 1 hour.

1 piece: 611 cal., 36g fat (10g sat. fat), 31mg chol., 234mg sod., 67g carb. (33g sugars, 3g fiber), 6g pro.

51 BERRIES WITH VANILLA CUSTARD

What a simple, delectable way to enjoy fresh raspberries. For a change, also try the custard with strawberries or peaches.

—Sarah Vasques, Milford, NH

PREP: 20 MIN. + CHILLING
MAKES: 4 SERVINGS

  1 cup half-and-half cream
  2 large egg yolks
  2 Tbsp. sugar
  2 tsp. vanilla extract
  2 cups fresh berries

1. In a small heavy saucepan, mix cream, egg yolks and sugar. Cook and stir over low heat until the mixture is just thick enough to coat a metal spoon, and a thermometer reads at least 160°. Do not allow to boil.
2. Transfer to a bowl; stir in the vanilla. Refrigerate, covered, until cold. Serve over fresh berries.

½ cup berries with ¼ cup sauce: 166 cal., 9g fat (5g sat. fat), 132mg chol., 34mg sod., 16g carb. (11g sugars, 4g fiber), 4g pro.
Diabetic exchanges: 1½ fat, ½ starch, ½ fruit.

GRILLED FRUIT PHYLLO TART

GRILLED FRUIT PHYLLO TART

This tart was a hit at a friend's baby shower. It reminds me of a fruit salad that my mother used to make with whipped topping and cream cheese. Everyone loves the flaky crust and the bright colors.
—Laura McAllister, Morganton, NC

PREP: 30 MIN. • **GRILL:** 10 MIN.
MAKES: 12 SERVINGS

- 3 Tbsp. butter, melted
- 4 tsp. canola oil
- 8 sheets phyllo dough (14x9-in. size)
- 1 large lemon
- 3 medium peaches, peeled and halved
- 2 cups large fresh strawberries, stems removed
- 4 slices fresh pineapple (½ in. thick)
- ⅓ cup packed brown sugar
- ½ tsp. salt
- ½ cup heavy whipping cream
- 1 pkg. (8 oz.) cream cheese, softened
- ⅓ cup confectioners' sugar
- 2 Tbsp. chopped fresh mint

1. Preheat oven to 400°. In a small bowl, mix butter and oil. Brush a 15x10x1-in. baking pan with some of the butter mixture. Place 1 sheet of phyllo dough into prepared pan; brush with butter mixture. Layer with 7 additional phyllo sheets, brushing each layer. (Keep the remaining phyllo covered with waxed paper and a damp towel to prevent it from drying out.) Bake 5-7 minutes or until golden brown (phyllo will puff up during baking). Cool completely.
2. Finely grate 1 Tbsp. lemon zest. Cut lemon crosswise in half; squeeze out the juice. In a large bowl, toss peaches, strawberries, pineapple, brown sugar, salt, lemon zest and juice. Remove the strawberries; thread onto 3 metal or soaked wooden skewers.
3. Place the fruit on oiled grill rack. Grill, covered, over medium heat 8-10 minutes for the pineapple slices and peaches; 4-5 minutes for the strawberries or until fruit is tender, turning once. Remove and set aside.
4. In a small bowl, beat cream until soft peaks form. In another bowl, beat cream cheese and confectioners' sugar until smooth. Fold in whipped cream. Spread over phyllo crust. Slice the grilled fruit; arrange over filling. Sprinkle with mint.
1 piece: 233 cal., 15g fat (8g sat. fat), 38mg chol., 216mg sod., 24g carb. (18g sugars, 2g fiber), 3g pro.

MANGO RICE PUDDING

Mangoes are my son's favorite fruit, so I was ecstatic to incorporate them into a healthy dessert. You can also use ripe bananas instead of mango, almond extract instead of vanilla, or regular milk in place of soy.
—Melissa McCabe, Victor, NY

PREP: 5 MIN. • **COOK:** 50 MIN.
MAKES: 4 SERVINGS

   2   cups water
   ¼   tsp. salt
   1   cup uncooked long grain brown
        rice
   1   medium ripe mango
   1   cup vanilla soy milk
   2   Tbsp. sugar
   ½   tsp. ground cinnamon
   1   tsp. vanilla extract
        Chopped peeled mango, optional

1. In a large heavy saucepan, bring water and salt to a boil; stir in the rice. Reduce heat; simmer, covered, 35-40 minutes or until water is absorbed and rice is tender.
2. Meanwhile, peel, seed and slice mango. Mash mango with a potato masher or fork.
3. Stir the milk, sugar, cinnamon and mashed mango into the rice. Cook, uncovered, on low 10-15 minutes longer or until the liquid is almost absorbed, stirring occasionally.
4. Remove from heat; stir in vanilla. Serve warm or cold, with chopped mango if desired.
1 cup: 275 cal., 3g fat (0 sat. fat), 0 chol., 176mg sod., 58g carb. (20g sugars, 3g fiber), 6g pro.

STRAWBERRY-HAZELNUT MERINGUE SHORTCAKES

🔵 STRAWBERRY-HAZELNUT MERINGUE SHORTCAKES

In early summer, the strawberry farms in our area open to the public for picking. These shortcakes really show off the big, juicy berries of our harvest.
—Barbara Estabrook, Appleton, WI

PREP: 25 MIN. • **BAKE:** 45 MIN. + COOLING
MAKES: 8 SERVINGS

   2   **large egg whites**
   ½   **cup sugar**
   ¼   **cup finely chopped hazelnuts**
   6   **cups fresh strawberries, hulled**
        and sliced
   4   **cups low-fat frozen yogurt**

1. Place egg whites in a small bowl; let stand at room temperature 30 minutes.
2. Preheat oven to 250°. Beat egg whites on medium speed until foamy. Gradually add sugar, 1 Tbsp. at a time, beating on high after each addition until sugar is dissolved. Continue beating until stiff glossy peaks form.
3. Using a measuring cup and spatula or an ice cream scoop, drop meringue into 8 even mounds on a parchment-lined baking sheet. With the back of a spoon, shape into 3-in. cups. Sprinkle with hazelnuts. Bake 45-50 minutes or until set and dry. Turn off oven (do not open oven door); leave the meringues in oven 1 hour. Remove from oven; cool completely on baking sheets. Remove meringues from paper.
4. Place 3 cups strawberries in a large bowl; mash slightly. Stir in remaining strawberries. Just before serving, top the meringues with the frozen yogurt and strawberries.
1 serving: 212 cal., 4g fat (1g sat. fat), 5mg chol., 74mg sod., 40g carb. (36g sugars, 3g fiber), 7g pro.

STAR-SPANGLED
LEMON ICEBOX PIE

STAR-SPANGLED LEMON ICEBOX PIE

With a little chill time, my no-bake lemon pie turns into a potluck superstar. My kids like to arrange the berries in the patriotic pattern.
—Lauren Katz, Ashburn, VA

PREP: 35 MIN. + CHILLING
MAKES: 8 SERVINGS

- 15 pecan shortbread cookies (about 8 oz.)
- 1 Tbsp. sugar
- 3 Tbsp. butter, melted

FILLING
- 8 oz. cream cheese, softened
- ½ cup mascarpone cheese
- 1 Tbsp. grated lemon zest
- ½ cup lemon juice
- 1 can (14 oz.) sweetened condensed milk
- 1 cup sliced fresh strawberries
- 1 cup fresh blueberries

1. Preheat oven to 350°. Place cookies and sugar in a food processor; process until cookies are ground. Add the melted butter; pulse just until combined. Press the mixture onto bottom and up sides of an ungreased 9-in. pie plate. Bake 15-20 minutes or until lightly browned. Cool completely on a wire rack.
2. In a large bowl, beat cream cheese, mascarpone cheese, lemon zest and lemon juice until smooth; gradually beat in milk.
3. Spread cream cheese mixture into the prepared crust. Refrigerate, covered, at least 4 hours or until filling is set. Top with berries before serving.
1 piece: 591 cal., 41g fat (20g sat. fat), 104mg chol., 310mg sod., 52g carb. (38g sugars, 1g fiber), 10g pro.

BERRY DREAM CAKE

I use cherry gelatin to give a boxed cake mix an eye-appealing marbled effect. It's so festive-looking. Top it with whatever fruit you like!
—Margaret McNeil, Germantown, TN

PREP: 15 MIN. + CHILLING
BAKE: 30 MIN. + CHILLING
MAKES: 15 SERVINGS

- 1 pkg. white cake mix (regular size)
- 1½ cups boiling water
- 1 pkg. (3 oz.) cherry gelatin
- 1 pkg. (8 oz.) cream cheese, softened
- 2 cups whipped topping
- 4 cups fresh strawberries, coarsely chopped

1. Prepare and bake the cake mix batter according to package directions, using a greased 13x9-in. baking pan.
2. In a small bowl, add boiling water to gelatin; stir 2 minutes to completely dissolve. Cool the cake on a wire rack 3-5 minutes. Using a wooden skewer, pierce holes in top of cake to within 1 in. of edge, twisting skewer gently to make slightly larger holes. Gradually pour gelatin over cake, being careful to fill each hole. Cool 15 minutes. Refrigerate, covered, 30 minutes.
3. In a large bowl, beat cream cheese until fluffy. Fold in whipped topping. Carefully spread over cake. Top with strawberries. Cover and refrigerate for at least 2 hours before serving.
1 piece: 306 cal., 16g fat (6g sat. fat), 54mg chol., 315mg sod., 37g carb. (22g sugars, 1g fiber), 5g pro.

RECIPE INDEX